Simón Bolívar

To the Supreme Leader
to the incomparable Hero
the terror of Iberia and the Fame of his Country,
to the unvanquished warrior
hostage of tyrants and protector of people,
to the Genius of the enterprise,
Serious in opposition and modest in exaltation
and
ever great
Simón Bolívar
liberator, president, and general of the army of the
Republic of Colombia

Testimony to Bolívar's veneration

SIMÓN BOLÍVAR
HISTORY AND MYTH

Michael Zeuske

Translated by Steven Rendall and Lisa Neal

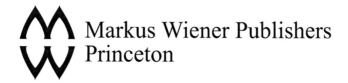
Markus Wiener Publishers
Princeton

Copyright © 2013 by Markus Wiener Publishers, Princeton, New Jersey, for the English language edition

Copyright © 2011 by Rotbuch Verlag, Berlin

The translation of this work was funded by Geisteswissenschaften International—Translation Funding for Humanities and Social Sciences from Germany, a joint initiative of the Fritz Thyssen Foundation, the German Federal Foreign Office, the collecting society VG WORT, and the Börsenverein des Deutschen Buchhandels (German Publishers & Booksellers Association).

All rights reserved. No part of this book may be reproduced or transmitted in any form or by any means, whether electronic or mechanical—including photocopying or recording—or through any information storage or retrieval system, without permission of the copyright owners.

For information, write to: Markus Wiener Publishers
231 Nassau Street, Princeton, NJ 08542
www.markuswiener.com

Library of Congress Cataloging-in-Publication Data

Zeuske, Michael.
 [Simón Bolívar, Befreier Südamerikas. English]
 Simón Bolívar : history and myth / Michael Zeuske ; translated from the German by Steven Rendall and Lisa Neal.
 p. cm.
 Translation of: Simón Bolívar, Befreier Südamerikas.
 Includes bibliographical references.
 ISBN 978-1-55876-567-2 (hardcover : alk. paper)
 ISBN 978-1-55876-568-9 (pbk. : alk. paper)
 1. Bolívar, Simón, 1783-1830. 2. Heads of state—South America—Biography.
 3. Latin America—History—Wars of Independence, 1806-1830. I. Title.
 F2235.3.Z4813 2012
 980'.02092—dc23
 [B]
     2012018861

Markus Wiener Publishers books are printed in the United States of America on acid-free paper and meet the guidelines for permanence and durability of the Committee on Production Guidelines for Book Longevity of the Council on Library Resources.

"Conceived by Miranda, organized by Bolívar."

—Miquel Izard

"The abolition of slavery was the key to Spanish-American independence."

—Hugh Thomas

CONTENTS

INTRODUCTION
Dimensions of the Bolívar Myth 1

CHAPTER I
Historical Foundations: Constructions of a Nation 11
    Elites without a Nation or a Myth 12
    Discourses of the Nation, Slave Revolts, and Caste Society 22
    Caudillos and Bolívar Revenants: Nineteenth-Century
        Experiments with the State 42
    The Conservative and the Revolutionary Bolívar in the
        "Age of Extremes" 46

CHAPTER II
Simón Bolívar: The Man and the Myth 51
    The Glorious Bolívar Family 51
    In Search of the Ancestors 53
    The Bolívars' Fortune 55
    The Conservative-Romantic Bolívar Myth 67
    From the "Marxist" to the "Democratic" Bolívar and Back 81

CHAPTER III
**Excursus: "Humboldt and Bolívar"—On a Conversation
That May Never Have Taken Place** 85
    Postscript, April 2012 97

INSTEAD OF A CONCLUSION
The "Chavist Bolívar" 99

NOTES 105

SELECT BIBLIOGRAPHY OF ENGLISH TEXTS
    ON SIMÓN BOLÍVAR 139

WORKS BY MICHAEL ZEUSKE ON BOLÍVAR,
    HUMBOLDT, MIRANDA, AND INDEPENDENCE 141

INTRODUCTION

Dimensions of the Bolívar Myth

Simón Bolívar is a hero. Even today he is surrounded by legends and stories, and he remains the subject of discourses, pictorial representations,[1] and architecture; material for literature and film; and a theme for political speeches and declarations. The Bolívar myth and the Bolívar cult have become, especially in Venezuela and parts of Colombia and Ecuador, a kind of ritualized civil religion, which is expressed in monumental narratives and rendered in pictures and statues.

At the origin of the phenomenon called Bolívarism (*Bolivarismo*) was the spoken and written word: Bolívar's speeches and addresses (*discursos*), writings (*escritos*), documents (*documentos*), decrees (*decretos*), letters (*cartas*), presidential messages (*mensajes*), and proclamations (*proclamaciones*) constitute several large archival collections (*colecciones*). The latter are not archives in the classical sense but rather editions of texts, the first of which was published between 1826 and 1829 and included more than thirty volumes.[2] But they are more than collections of documents; they are archives that constitute an official institutionalization of the myth.

However, in the area where Bolívarism had its greatest impact, in northern South America and the Caribbean, there was and still is a vibrant culture of orality and physical performance that may be even more important than these written documents. Today, texts, oral traditions, performative speech, and gesture still stand in a close and very productive relationship. One of the most important—perhaps *the* most important—bases for this are transcriptions of direct speech, that is, of apparently simple conversations between two speakers that derive from real situations or are perceived by literati as "authentic." As Bolívar's texts and archive spread, these speech situations reenter orality and constantly produce new configurations of the myth.

Marble monuments to Bolívar are found in all parts of Venezuela and in most world capitals.[3] For many years Vienna and London have each had one, and soon there will be others in Bonn and Berlin (where there is already a rather ugly statue of Bolívar in the library of the former Ibero-American Institute). Naturally, Hamburg, Germany's only Atlantic city, has its own Bolívar, in the Bolívar Park in Hamburg-Harvestehude, and a gigantic equestrian statue of Bolívar stands at the south entrance to New York's Central Park.

The Bolívar cult, in contrast to the narrative, oral, discursive, and visual myth, consists essentially of ritualized acts that initially served to found the state. Today, they serve as a kind of profane theater of institutions that confers legitimacy on state, national, cultural, memorial, sporting, and military events. Other rituals performed in the presence of statues and busts of Bolívar at memorial events such as conferences and international meetings belong in the same thematic area.[4] Scholars have given very little attention to specific historical acts and rituals of the Bolívar cult, even though the founding father of Venezuelan research on Bolívar, Germán Carrera Damas, analyzed the Bolívar myth in his book *El culto a Bolívar*[5] (*The Bolívar Cult*).[6]

Behind the nationalist myth and cult, with its Bolívar archives and marble monuments, there is much that is hardly visible for foreigners. In the rural-influenced cultures of Venezuela and Colombia, the universal and cosmopolitan complex of myth and cult rests on a very broad basis communicated mainly through oral media: performance, gestures, narratives, songs, and tales. The "people's Bolívar" emerged chiefly after the end of the Páez era (c. 1848) when a broad segment of the population was disappointed by the result of the civil war and by the transition from the colonial and national eras to Independencia. This Independencia under Bolívar, translated in the wider sense as "independence movement," took place between 1810 and 1830. But the break with Spain continued to trigger struggles for equality, freedom, a republic, and citizenship that often continued well into the 1880s.[7]

The "people's Bolívar" justified the protests and battles against the renewed domination of the estate- and slaveholding oligarchies that had been attempting since 1815 (under the Spanish general Pablo Morillo), and especially between 1821 and 1830, to consolidate the old order with or without foreign colonialism. This conservative reconstruction was most boldly challenged by the Venezuelan peasant general Ezequiel Zamora (1817–1860) and during the many rebellions that took place in the Llanos grasslands on the northern and western banks of the Orinoco River in the course of the nineteenth century. The protest is most easily discernible in the aural culture of the Llanos (narratives and songs) and also perhaps in naive-figural arts and crafts (altars and figures of the María Lionza religion[8]) or in the oral versions of the history of *Independencia* and Bolívar (which was first put into writing in the middle of the nineteenth century).[9]

The myth plays an important role in the local literatures as well.[10] In only two hundred years, the Bolívar myth has gone through several stylistic transformations, from Empire to Romantic, Costumbrist, positivist, Marxist, modern, and postmodern—the myth of myth.[11]

The message connected with the political icon Bolívar and his myth is relatively simple: it is the great story of the hero, of an exceptional individual, the liberator Simón Bolívar, who between 1819 and 1825, by sheer courage and resolution, ended Spain's domination over its colonies in America from Panama in the north to Peru in the south, and thereby liberated a whole continent, South America. And he was so noble and expressed so many good and great ideas in a form ready for print that he still remains an unparalleled model whose ideas have only to be realized. Thus today, under Hugo Chávez, Bolívar is extolled as the model for a continental union of the countries of South America against those to the north. Bolívar also truly believed he could make Great Colombia—a state consisting of the modern-day areas of Panama, Ecuador, Colombia, and Venezuela that existed from 1819 to 1830 and was even larger than those states are today—the "heart of the world." That is the great official history of Bolívar and the Bolívar myth.

The mulatto Bolívar in a painting by Alfredo Rodriguez (Haiti, 1816).

The oral versions of the myth emphasize above all the Bolívar of the battle for equality and agrarian reform and against slavery, mainly by creating a colored Bolívar and thus alluding to his African-Venezuelan ancestors. The Bolívar resembling a mulatto with a dark-skinned face and kinky hair is also a feature of his representation as an altar figure in the María Lionza cult. Another version of the cult sees Bolívar in the Indio tradition of the rebellious and warlike chieftain Guaicaipuro.[12]

The official state myth of Bolívar was produced by his companions in arms, his adjutant Daniel F. O'Leary, historians, and sociologists—in cooperation with the myth-building power of the popular imagination, which created the Bolívar of equality and the emancipation of slaves. In between, there is the Bolívar of the intellectuals and literati—between Teresa de la Parra and Gabriel Garcia Márquez, one might say.

At least since the second centennial of Independencia in 2010, the official myth of Bolívar has also been washing in great waves over television screens and feature pages in European periodicals. Interest began to grow in Germany as well, especially since the Liberator had long since been systematically developed as the symbol of a new left-wing self-image.[13] Therefore I have decided not to write a "new Bolívar" or a history of the colonial crisis and the independence movements "without Bolívar" (the latter is urgently needed but is also very difficult to achieve) but rather to explain the Bolívar myth in the framework of its sphere of influence, the history of Venezuela and northern South America, including the Caribbean. My goal is to examine not only the myth's power to produce results, but also its *true* history and the *real* origin of the protagonists involved.

In Latin America, myths—including the Bolívar myth—are associated with very dynamic processes and have historical roots and real backgrounds that are either not known or often overlooked in Europe. As such, the myth is neither bad nor unscientific. On the contrary, in the contexts of their development and in their legitimating intentions, myths are simply historical phenomena that can be traced back to what Michel Foucault calls discursive series with real conditions of emergence, apparatuses, and assertions.

To illustrate this by means of an example: in Germany, everyone, literally *everyone*, who is concerned with Simón Bolívar and the independence of Spanish America thinks first of the phrase "Humboldt and Bolívar." This generally leads automatically to the following line of thought: *Wasn't Humboldt a brilliant super-scientist who was already thinking globally? And didn't this genius talk with the hero Bolívar? Aren't there even pictures and sketches of the two heroes meeting in Paris in 1804 and on Vesuvius in 1805? Thus Humboldt must have given Simón Bolívar the idea of fighting for the noble goal of independence!*

This myth did not derive solely from the fact that Germans like to think of themselves as the nation of poets and thinkers. It can be traced back to the extreme need for legitimacy felt after 1830 by the states that had formerly been part of Spanish America. To legitimate the elites of these new states, it was urgently necessary to make some of Alexander von Humboldt's splendor shine on the rulers who had, during the civil wars around 1830 connected with the independence movement, sought without exception to create a state order that only barely concealed the fact that the true goal was to reconstruct the old colonial economic and social orders. In reality, Humboldt took hardly any interest in Bolívar, who before 1810 was, to exaggerate a bit, a kind of rock star. In 1804, Simón Bolívar was a world-weary young millionaire and a skirt chaser par excellence who came from a distant exotic colony, often appeared in literary salons, consumed coffee-table books by the currently fashionable *philosophes*, and was so tired of life that he walked from Rome to Naples as a kind of therapy. In the Bolívar myth, this flighty, excessively nervous, and at the same time somewhat slow young Bolívar is a hero who does not yet know his own potential. The encounter between Bolívar and Humboldt in Paris in 1804 is seen as an awakening. All statements regarding the meeting of the two men are based on what Humboldt is supposed to have told Daniel F. O'Leary in 1853, when he was over eighty years old: that he recalled having "had much intercourse with Bolívar" in 1804.[14] This is a classic ex post facto construction, because around 1850 everyone, including Humboldt, was familiar with the early Bolívar myth. As was suitable for a tragic hero, Bolívar had died young in Santa Marta in 1830, on his way into exile. He was only forty-seven years old.

As we have already seen, in Latin America, this premise—"Humboldt awakened Bolívar"—served an important function in legitimating the new republican order under the domination of the indigenous elites, who liked to vaunt their close relationships with the world-famous scientist Humboldt and with "modern" Europe. In fact, with its "republican" form of government, Latin America was far more progressive than the monarchical states of Europe, although the republican states of the former Spanish America were for the most part led by extremely conservative social and economic elites. This conservatism in Latin America is most clearly seen by examining the key issue of slavery: between 1815 and 1819, efforts to abolish slavery were made in several places in order to prevent slaves from becoming a source of recruits for enemy armies.[15] However, after 1820—with exceptions such as Mexico and Chile—the old relationships were covertly reestablished, precisely because in the area where the Bolívar myth thrived, the government had for the most part been taken over by slaveholders and plantation owners. The fight to abolish slavery was later waged in battles up to about 1860 (in Cuba and Brazil, slavery was abolished only in 1886 and 1888, respectively). However, the new forms of government established between 1820 and 1830 proved to be extremely important. Since in their rebellions to achieve autonomy the local elites had to rely on the republic, the new form of government made possible a republicanism from below and a relatively open political battle for equality, freedom, and democracy.[16]

On the German side, the constructions of "Simón Bolívar and Alexander von Humboldt"[17] generally emerged from scholarly interests and were used for diplomatic or ideological reasons to add a South American dimension to the Humboldt myth.[18]

In recent decades, historians have developed various methods for analyzing the construction of myths. One method is deconstructive; it has the disadvantage of remaining largely on the level of texts, images, and monuments; often, whole books deal with only one text, one person, or one picture.[19] Another method, which is in my view more promising, recognizes myths as important phenomena in the history of ideas and discourses (in Foucault's sense), and sheds light on the conditions of their emergence, their real origin, and their function. The analysis must thus be historical. It must also take into account the fact that myths have social, structural, economic, and political causes and that they exercise functions in real history. On this basis the spiritual, cultural, medial, and artistic aspects of myths can be investigated. Beyond historical recognition, it seems to me methodologically important to connect myths with a kind of anthropological microhistory and social history. This means connecting myths back to life histories, to people who really lived, and who populate the microstructures and thus fill the macrostructures (the South American continent, the Caribbean, the Atlantic area, Europe and America, the "West") with individual acts.

By connecting (*religare*) medial processes to social reality, I will offer an interpretation of the history of the Independencia from the point of view of the life of Simón José Antonio de la Santísima Trinidad Bolívar y Palacios (1783–1830). This will be above all a history of Venezuela, but it will also deal with northern South America and with the question as to why, in the countries in which the Bolívar myth is most influential, there has still never been a social revolution—either under reactionary auspices, as in the case of the conservative revolution that led to the development of the sugar economy and mass slavery in Cuba, or under revolutionary-democratic conditions.

To anticipate one of the results of my investigation: Simón Bolívar was one of those most responsible for this—on the one hand, in his role as a military Jacobin and, on the other hand, as the embodiment of the continuity of the old colonial elites—despite or precisely because of his military radicalism and his shrewd understanding of the problems of his times. In particular, however, the conservative Bolívar myth and the massive Bolívar cult developed by the respective ruling elites around 1870 helped prevent a profound social upheaval. Moreover, this fact makes all versions of the Bolívar myth ambivalent.[20]

In investigating "Simón Bolívar: History and Myth," I want to avoid taking the Liberator as a proxy for the political and social processes of the Independencia, as is commonly done in many studies on the independence movement. Instead, my goal is to produce a critical history of the crisis of the colonial state and of the wars that were fought over the new state between 1810 and 1870. In addition, I will seek to analyze Simón Bolívar as an individual, as the Bolívar myth also claims to do. My observations are, however, not invented but are based on two central points of view, the construction of a nation and the history of slavery, of the Llaneros and other large oppressed groups in the colonial period, and of the *pardos* who constituted most of the colored population. Their descendants also shaped the image of modern Venezuela.

In the crisis of the Spanish Empire and colonialism following the Atlantic revolutions (1775–1850), the pardos were the chief actors in the lengthy civil wars. There is a close connection between the history of the Independencia and the history of slaves, even if the elites of their time and many current historians have minimized the problem of slavery and Independencia. The control over slaves and over the part of the population that had slave ancestors was one of the most important factors driving the independence movement of the Creole elites, as Humboldt already very lucidly noted around 1800.[21]

In this book, quotations from texts in other languages appear in English translation, and are given in the original in the notes. I have deliberately not abstained from giving references for all quotations and written sources, as well as their traces in the text archeology, in extensive notes. Every reader can examine these references to determine for himself or herself which paths myth constructions follow. They show that historical research is more exciting than any detective story.

Leipzig, Vienna, Caracas, Havana, Murcia, Cologne, and Liblar
End of 2008 to June 2011

CHAPTER I

Historical Foundations: Constructions of a Nation

By the term "nation," we generally mean a community of people with homogeneous characteristics (language, tradition, culture, history, etc.) living in a specific territory.
A broader interpretation emphasizes the possibilities of change in a political space that includes groups with differing characteristics. The latter is true of Venezuela, where the Conquista (as a partial process of early globalization), colonization, and revolutions all contributed to the development of a nation.[1]

Before the 1860s, elites probably had never been able to convert the idiosyncrasies of a community into a practical domestic politics. It can, of course, be argued that movements in this direction, such as relatively clearly defined territories, relatively homogeneous subjects, and common cultural elements, can already be observed in some of the small monarchies of the Middle Ages or the Early Modern age. In Europe, Portugal, Castile, Denmark, and England might be mentioned. However, the homogeneity sought, which was always more ideal than real, quickly disappeared from view as a result of the European colonial expansion and the globalization connected with the history of these early modern nations. Large states that established empires (such as the Holy Roman Empire, the French, Polish-Lithuanian, and Russian empires, or the colonial empires that proceeded from expansion) subsequently discovered the unifying power of the idea of a nation—if they survived the early modern period at all as a political territory. At the other extreme, in smaller states or city-states, most of which were commercial communities, the notion of a nation or nationalism played only a minor role. More crucial were translocality and nepotism among the elites, so that wealth and power counted for more than any real or imagined commonality.

In the Western hemisphere and especially in Europe, it is still assumed that the state conceived as a territorial receptacle for subsequent nations was in fact a product exported by Europe.[2] This may hold true for an ideological concept of the nation, for the state as a way of organizing dominance and power, but only to a very limited extent. In the regions of Africa, America, and Asia (especially in the Arab-Persian-Islamic area and in China), states and empires often appeared long before they developed in Europe. However, these were not communities configured as nations.

Elites without a Nation or a Myth

The question of how a nation develops arises differently in areas of the world in which, before 1500, there was no state structure, and domination had been institutionalized in only a rudimentary way. This was especially true on the Atlantic coasts of North and South America, as well as in the Caribbean. As a geo-historical space, the latter area is now often called the Gran Caribe, and includes the Greater and Lesser Antilles, all the other island groups, and all the coasts between St. Augustine, Florida, in the north and Santo Tomás de Guyana in the south (often still called the "wild coasts," from the Guyanas to the mouth of the Orinoco and, in some cases, even as far as the mouth of the Amazon). Here the Iberian captains, sailing in search of goods to trade, precious metals, and luxury items, first landed on islands that had been settled by many peoples, tribes, and groups belonging to two major cultures: the Arawaks and the Caribs. Only among the Taino, a seafaring Arawak people with its center on the island of Bohio (which Columbus called La Española and today comprises Haiti and the Dominican Republic), was ruled by chieftains already institutionalized in a definite hereditary succession and territoriality. Since the Tainos must have recognized that the foreigners would come back (Columbus's second expedition), they made alliances with Columbus and his Andalusian and Castilian crews. In return, this meant that all enemies of the Tainos were almost automatically enemies of the Castilians. There was a series of further conflicts and connections that structured the history of these communities and still influenced them at the beginning of colonial history.

First, the conflicts. During the Middle Ages, the Tainos, coming with their chieftains from the east (via the Lesser Antilles) and from the west (via the coasts of Central America), had settled on the Greater Antilles. Around 1500, they were confronted by hostile attacks by Caribs arriving in canoes. A whole series of Taino chieftains had thus also made arrangements with the Spaniards out of fear of the savage Carib warriors. In early writings by Columbus and the Spaniards, the Caribs are described as cannibals, in terms that are still horrifying.[3] At the time, this stylized image served mainly to explain why, despite the Crown's prohibition, certain groups of Indios (borrowing the Spanish term to avoid confusion of "Indians" with natives of India) could be enslaved as new subjects.

This brings us to the connections. Using seagoing canoes, both the Tainos and the Caribs had constructed trade networks in the Caribbean area. In this way, they exchanged goods—especially salt and dyestuffs, but also prisoners of war (slaves). From the outset, the Spaniards made use of these networks for their own purposes.

Shortly after the arrival of the Spaniards, the "demographic catastrophe" struck the Indios. Friend and foe fell victim to the diseases imported along with the European livestock. The new ways of living and working added to the catastrophe. The Taino community was the first to suffer the consequences of European colonial expansion and the unrestrained violence of the Conquista. On La Española, colonists established a settlement with forced labor (*repartimiento, encomienda*), new ecclesiastical and state institutions, and slavery (*naboria*). For about thirty years, the island was the center of Iberian colonization in the area, which from 1507 on was designated on some maps of the world in the Ptolemaic tradition by the technical term "America." Around 1510, when Spaniards—initially, Dominican monks like Montesino and Las

Casas—revealed the scandalous annihilation of the Tainos, present-day Venezuela was brought into play.

In contrast to the island of La Hispaniola, which the Spaniards occupied, the enormous land mass to the south and southwest, where the Andalusian ship captains and their Italian financiers were seeking a passage to India, was called Tierra Firme (the mainland). Because the workforce used by the Spaniards was dying off, the part of Tierra Firme directly south of La Española became the raiding ground for professional slave hunters. In addition, allied Indios (the Guayqueriés) told the colonizers about the pearl beds on the eastern edge of the country, around the island Cubagua. At least spatially, we are thus in the region of modern Venezuela.

The Spanish Crown gave the greater part of modern Venezuela and part of modern Colombia to the Welsers,[4] a German family of businessmen and bankers to which it owed money. On the other hand, it sought above all to settle the coasts in the eastern part of the region, handing them over to the Dominicans as a missionary area. Both efforts—the Welser settlement (1528–1556) and the missionary work of the Dominicans—failed as a result of the conflict between slave hunters and Indio peoples. The Caribs in particular put up a massive and violent resistance. The tribes retreated from the coast, so that the first attempts to establish settlements succeeded only on the island of Cubagua in east and in Coro on the north coast of modern Venezuela.

When in these centers of Iberian settlement, which still included Indio women and slaves, a first generation of descendants of the European conquistadors and Indio women reached maturity (around 1550–60), there was a new wave of Iberian-mestizo expansion. In the valleys of the coastal Andes, settlements emerged, including Caracas, and the other cities and villages that were to ensure the connection through the Andes to New Granada (now Colombia). There, on the basis of Indio forms of rule, the New Kingdom of Granada was founded in 1538. Its center was the town of Bacata (now Bogotá). Soon, at first because of the mass plundering of Indio graves, gold and other precious metals were found and sent back to Europe. The pearl beds around Cubagua in the east were exhausted, and the regions of modern Venezuela and the Guyanas were reduced to the rank of peripheries of war and borderlands. Basically, these regions retained an imperial interest only because the attention of the English—under the command of Walter Raleigh—had been attracted since 1570 to the Guyanas as a border territory between the Castilian and Portuguese colonial settlements. The English were followed by the Dutch, who were initially interested in the great natural salt pans at Araya in the eastern part of modern Venezuela.

Regions formerly ruled by the Indios became, as provinces, territorial units of the Spanish monarchy. In reality, the colonial Tierra Firme, which consisted of a few shabby settlements and early towns with their respective hinterlands, became a collection of poorly administered provinces that had hardly any relation to one another. Six of the larger settlements were given charters and became centers for provincial administration: on the coast of the Caribbean, Coro, Maracaibo, Caracas (with its roadstead harbor La Guaira), and Cumaná; just off the coast, Mérida, which secured the Andes connection with New Granada; and Santo Tomé de la Guyana, which protected the mouth of the Orinoco. Ecclesiastical organization and the administration of justice were commonly shifted back and forth between Santo Domingo (on La Española) and Bogotá (in New Granada), along with the administrative affiliations of individual provinces. The fortresses on the coasts of the Caribbean and on the Orinoco were "grant areas" (*situados*) of the Spanish Empire. Thus not even administratively was there even a trace of a sense of community.

In addition, there were other divisions, some of which are still operative. In the cities, the few families of the first conquistadors, which survived exclusively through marriage politics, withdrew defensively into a caste system in which all others, categorized in terms of their "mixed blood" were considered *castas bajas* (lower castes)—Indios, blacks, and coloreds, of course, but also "poor whites," most of whom came from the Canary Islands to the cities on the Caribbean coast. Venezuela continued to be an area of war and raiding for groups hunting Indios, especially in the east, where there was bitter hatred between Spaniards and mestizos on the one hand and proud Carib warriors (and also slave hunters) on the other. In the center of modern Venezuela, beyond the coastal cordillera, and in the enormous Llanos plains, huge herds of escaped and half-wild livestock were formed, consisting especially of horses (a kind of Caribbean mustang), cattle, asses, and mules. This border culture, which soon incorporated military deserters, criminals from the provincial cities, and fugitive slaves, was basically Indio. It was based on the large livestock the Europeans had brought to America and on hunting half-wild animals. In the east, English and Dutch colonists pressed forward into the border area between the Portuguese and Spanish colonial areas and made alliances with Caribbean tribes.

Essentially, the provinces in the territory of modern Venezuela served solely to secure a single harbor in present-day Colombia: Cartagena de Indias, founded in 1532. In Spain's developing trade, using fleets of transport ships convoyed by galleons—the so-called Flotas y Galeones system—Cartagena became, along with the complicated connection via the Portobello-Panama isthmus, one of South America's principal harbors for the exportation of precious metals and the importation of African slaves. A ship from the Spanish fleet visited Venezuela's cities at most once a year. Often years went by without any official exchange with the home country. The settlers resorted to smuggling, piracy, and border and raiding economies (*entradas*) that involved chiefly the illegal capture of Indio slaves. Provinces that were in themselves peripheral nonetheless lay at the center of the Atlantic facade of South America and profited from the transatlantic slave trade. It was of no importance whether the slave traders and ship captains operated with or without the permission of a government. When they wanted to sail from West Africa to America and its gold-exporting harbors (like Cartagena), they had to go north from Cabo São Roque, the easternmost point of modern Brazil, along the 4,000-kilometer-long Atlantic coast of South America. There also lay the Venezuelan cities of Cumaná, Caracas/La Guaira, Coro, and Maracaibo.

The numerous slave smugglers soon came to be called "Portuguese." Among them were European Portuguese but also colored and black Portuguese from Portugal's spheres of influence in Africa (Luanda in Angola, Congo, Elmina in modern-day Ghana, and also the harbors and islands in the area of the present Senegambian Confederation and Sierra Leone). Portuguese Sephardim had also settled on the peripheries of the Portuguese trade empire and established extensive Atlantic and global trade relations. Finally, all the smugglers and traders roaming the Atlantic without a monopoly, whom we would today probably term Atlantic Creoles, were called "Portuguese."[5]

It may have been one of these "Portuguese" who, after a slave-smuggling voyage from Africa to Veracruz (another great monopoly harbor of Spanish America in the Caribbean, in New Spain, now Mexico), took with him on his next smuggling trip from Luanda to Veracruz the knowledge of the great demand for cocoa in the Viceroyalty of New Spain (where the Aztecs had already cultivated cocoa beans). In the provinces of modern Venezuela and in the Guyanas, the Indios had discovered an exceptional, very sweet cocoa bean and used it for over a century. Thus emerged a gigantic smuggling economy based on the principle of "cocoa beans (and precious metals) in exchange for African slaves" and luxury goods, which quickly brought wealth and status to the settler elites in the coastal cities. The backcountry economy also benefited from the Atlantic trade in human bodies in exchange for precious metals and cocoa beans.

Many mestizos and mulattos took part in the development of the cocoa bean economy and smuggling in the hot coastal valleys and flood plains of modern Venezuela. However, the elites had made rapid use of Crown privileges to appropriate the best land in the form of great estates (latifundia), on which they established haciendas (cocoa and indigo plantations) or *hatos* (cattle ranches) on the northern borders of the Llanos. But in the exportation of Spanish America's cocoa beans, and also in that of tobacco (Barinas tobacco), which was just beginning, there were also profits to be made by colored non-elites, which often operated as smugglers or, acting as slave hunters, provided the workforce. The Dutch promptly got involved as well. In 1634, with the help of Sephardic and Cuban pirates, they conquered the ABC Islands off the coast of Venezuela in order to participate in the brisk smuggling business. Curaçao, which was actually a completely infertile and dry sand island, was transformed into a prominent platform for trade in slaves and smuggled goods. Subsequently there was more and more "Dutch" cocoa in Europe: "It was Sephardic Jews from Amsterdam who first brought cocoa beans to Europe and introduced the production of chocolate."[6]

In this smuggling trade, the cities of Venezuela were all oriented toward the outside; internally they carried on theft and raiding economies. They also participated in smuggling cattle and leather, which deepened the gap between them and the Llaneros, the hunting peoples of the Orinoco plains, and the Caribs or led to conflicts with the Dutch and Portuguese of expanding Brazil and with the slave settlements of fugitive Maroons, Quilombos, and cumbes. The urban elites also battled each other for predominance in the smuggling system. Caracas/La Guaira had the advantage of being situated in a way that protected it from attacks. The city lies only twenty-five kilometers from the ocean, behind a coastal cordillera that is like a fortress wall and is more than two thousand meters high. The establishment of an Episcopal see in Coro, Venezuela's "first city," also gave Caracas a head start. For the most part, the bishops preferred to reside in the "city of eternal spring" rather than in the dry, hot city of Coro. Agents of the first institution that included all the provinces, the Inquisition, also operated from Caracas.[7]

The designation "Venezuela" (little Venice), coined by the first captains in the time of Columbus on the basis of the pile dwellings built by the Indio peoples on Lake Maracaibo, was increasingly transferred to the province of Caracas, so that on early maps the present name of the country often appears as the Provincia de Caracas o de Venezuela.[8] Smuggling and slave trading brought wealth. With the trade in tobacco and cocoa beans, the elites of the periphery created one of the earliest Atlantic export economies, effectively bypassing the Spanish Crown's claim to hold a monopoly on trade. The families of the first Conquistadors were still more exclusive than before. Their women acquired the privilege of going to church wearing a gold and silver embroidered shawl, the *manta*—hence the term *mantuanos*. We also find them called collectively *grandes cacaos* (big cocoa beans). Despite their opposition to centralization ("free trade") the leading mantuanos got positions in the Spanish administration or became treasurers, lawyers, university professors, or officers in the militia or the army—not least in order to conceal and protect their smuggling activities. Often they paid enormous sums to buy Spanish titles of nobility for themselves. Bound together by nepotism and endogamy, the result was the development of a small white elite that was extremely proud of its caste. Its members called themselves *españoles americanos* (American Spaniards) and were concerned with the purity of their blood (*limpieza de sangre*). All the lower classes were considered as being of lower *calidad* (quality). "Objective" criteria for this often racist evaluation included—in addition to phenotypical characteristics (skin, hair, shape of the head, lips, nose, etc.), which were, however, seldom written down—the place (Africa or a settlement of mulattos and blacks) or kind (illegitimate) of birth.[9] Nevertheless, this did not prevent the male mantuanos from keeping female slaves, former slaves, or free colored women as lovers and producing many children with them. For one thing, their sons—called mestizos, pardos, or mulattos—were needed as overseers, haulers, guards, ship captains, sailors, and traffickers in the activities of smuggling and slave trading. The latter were often the real bosses. The vast majority of the pardos and even former slaves derived both a position and an income from smuggling. This resulted on the one hand in a strong orientation toward free trade, informality, social ascension, and adaptation to the norms of the elites. On the other hand, the caste pride of the mantuanos gave rise to a series of very serious conflicts.

The economic boom brought with it a major immigration, especially from the Canary Islands, so that even today Venezuela is often called the "eighth island" of the Canaries.[10] In the population of Venezuela, colored people, who soon became the majority, were called collectively pardos. People from the Canary Islands (about 10 to 12 percent) were considered white and Spanish but were soon and specifically categorized in the caste system as *blancos de orilla* (poor whites) and *isleños* (islanders). In contrast, the mantuanos, about 500 or 600 families around 1800, constituted at that time no more than 0.5 percent of a total population of between 900,000 and 1,000,000 people.

Despite all the ritual subordination that the mantuanos displayed with regard to the Crown and its principal agents in the colony, to the provincial governors and the captains general, most of whom were Spaniards, there was nonetheless a central problem—the claim to monopoly made by the Crown and the colonial bureaucracy. The Crown had never formally authorized "Atlanticization," that is, unimpeded access to smuggling and the trade in African slaves across the Atlantic (one of the main reasons for what Marx called "original accumulation" in the British colonial area). It is true that the nearby city of Cartagena became, between 1580 and 1620, the most important worldwide center for trade in precious metals and slaves. But there, the Spanish Crown and the Inquisition were able to regain control over the closely interwoven nexus of smuggling and slave trading. Many of those involved in these activities withdrew completely into informal trading in Jamaica, Curaçao, and other smuggling centers where the connections with Venezuela functioned.[11] The country was one of the most important smuggling areas for the British as well as the Dutch (it was also a center for Catholic missionaries, who were probably also involved in smuggling).[12]

At the beginning of the eighteenth century, the Crown granted a monopoly on cocoa bean exports (and sales in Mexico and Spain) to two Crown companies. Tobacco was also attracting more and more attention from economic policy makers in Madrid. The mantuanos often spoke and wrote in opposition to the hated monopoly, but because of their positions, political pressure at the court in Madrid, and their family connections with the new monopoly companies (especially in the Real Compañia Guipuzcoana de Caracas, based in San Sebastian in the Basque country), they were well placed to take advantage of it. The armed ships and the inspectors of monopoly companies were chiefly concerned to hunt down the small-scale smugglers.

Between 1630 and 1750, the smuggling business operated to the satisfaction of all, but toward the middle of the eighteenth century, serious excesses and uprisings occurred. These are often misinterpreted from the point of view of present-day historiography as the first awakening of nationalism. In reality, they were antitax and anticentralist rebellions and uprisings against the Crown's monopoly policy. However, inherent in them was a basic free-trade tendency that Venezuela never abandoned, even under the many dictatorships of the nineteenth and twentieth centuries.

Following Spain's defeat in the Seven Years' War, in which it was involved for five years (1759–1763), the Spanish monarchy agreed, after long debates, to genuine reforms "on both sides of the Atlantic." Not only Cuba but also and especially the periphery of Venezuela became proving grounds for the Bourbons' reforms.[13] Starting in 1776, Caracas, which had been been a rather informal midpoint of the jumble of ill-managed provinces, received in quick succession a series of institutions that elevated it over the other provinces and made it a true center. The post of captain general (who was responsible for military defense) was combined with that of governor of the province of Caracas, and the reformers appointed an intendant responsible for economics and for equipping the troops in all provinces. In addition, a trade council and a supreme court (*audiencia*) were created, and an archbishopric was established with its see in Caracas. The only university in the region had been founded in Caracas in 1730. Thus what had been merely a loose conglomerate of provinces—Mérida, Barinas (with Apure), Maracaibo, Margarita, Coro, Cumaná, Trinidad (until 1797), Guyana, and Caracas—was now formally united under the leadership of Caracas and protected by institutions.

In a kind of ideal history, the process of building a state and a nation might have begun at that point—and this might have been the dream of many heads of the mantuano family clans. But in real history, it would take about 120 to 150 rebellions, revolts, caudillo conflicts, and civil wars, as well as dictatorships and revolutions, between 1810 and 1908 (and afterward, a series of military putsches and further dictatorships) in order to even approach the construction and maintenance of a state territory. The consolidation of the state and the nation is still going on today. So far as the state is concerned, Venezuela, and Colombia as well, with its Llano provinces (Araure), have recently increasingly lost sovereignty again over marginal areas like Estado Apure or Guyana's border regions—or never had it in the first place.

Regarding the historical foundations of nation building, this long excursus on colonial history is intended to show that many of the striking ruptures, antagonisms, and differences in mentalities stem from this period. Neither the continuing structural (and overt) violence nor the deeply rooted racism that solidified at that time could be interrupted or even abolished by the period of Independencia, usually represented as the phase during which the nation was formed. On the contrary: violence and racism grew more acute through the installation of European models of the state, whether that of the imperial "Nation on both sides of the Atlantic" after 1770 or the republican state with a liberal constitution after 1819. These constructions and the social communities that emerged with them around the figure of the Spaniard and his language excluded the "castes" of slaves and "savage Indios."

Discourses of the Nation, Slave Revolts, and Caste Society

From about 1760 on, discourses about the nation were conducted in several ways. After the Seven Years' War, the Spanish Empire was finally forced to groom new elites that could advance a process of reform in accord with Enlightenment norms. These elites were initially formed primarily in Spain itself. The Bourbon reforms known as "Charles III's reforms" affected Spanish America chiefly from 1763 to 1788. During that time, Venezuela underwent the aforementioned process of centralization that made Caracas the center of the colonial area.

Only during the next phase of the Bourbon reforms, carried out under King Charles IV (1788–1808), did it occur to Spain to include the local elites in America as well. The goal was to form out of Las Españas (the Spains, not Spain) an imperial "Nation on both sides of the Atlantic,"[14] as the motto put it. Despite enormous problems, the Spanish monarchy "composed" of different territories was in this matter far more successful than its main competitor, the British Empire (which had recently had to accept the secession of the thirteen colonies that later became the United States). The Spanish kingdom was also better off in this respect than its ally France with its centralistic Bourbons. Above all, in Spanish America the use of the word "nation" to designate a new program for a transatlantic community (*nación*) competed with a long-established term.

Starting in the seventeenth century, black slaves who had been transported directly from Africa to South America were termed *de nación*. Initially, the same still held for a concept of community that was, after 1830, increasingly used as a political concept designating the "white" elites born in America who had just split off from Spain: the *criollos* (Creoles). During the whole colonial period up to 1830, the term "Creole" was used more or less pejoratively for slaves born in America. In addition, starting in 1776 there was some talk coming from the north and then, after 1789, from Europe about an anticolonial nation and a revolutionary nation "of the Third Estate," whose supporters saw themselves as citizens rather than as subjects of a crown.

The mantuanos, with a few exceptions, were completely opposed to the new concepts of community. The new elites created by imperial reforms were a threat to the mantuanos' privileges and their factual independence. On the other hand, Caracas's advantage over the other provincial cities suited the central elites of Venezuela just fine, but it triggered serious conflicts with the elites of Maracaibo, Coro, Cumaná, and Guyana. The increased advancement of pardos, who had risen in society, also led to conflicts. Since 1795 they had been able to purchase for large sums of money various privileges that had earlier been reserved for mantuanos. The latter were also hostile to the new militias of free colored people and blacks (*milicias de pardos y morenos*), which outnumbered the "white" units by a ratio of ten to one.

This relatively successful phase of reform in Spain and in its colonial kingdoms, which were legally affiliated with Castile (as *reinos ultramarinos*), was overshadowed by an event unprecedented in world history: the slave revolution in Santo Domingo/Haiti (1791–1803). As a radical upheaval, the slave revolution was unique. It manifested itself in cruel internal and external wars, including wars against the three superpowers of the time: Great Britain, France, and Spain. With independence and the abolition of slavery, the revolution also produced a new *ethnos*: slaves, free blacks, and colored people became Haitians and were also called *nègres* (blacks) in the new constitution.[15] For Venezuela's elites, this revolution at first consisted only of news reports. But these reports were far more real than the other discourses of revolution and nation. Between Venezuela, Santo Domingo, the Caribbean, and the other French colonies, there were thousands of connections: trade routes, travels, visits, family ties, escape routes used by slaves, epistolary correspondence, and the like. A much larger number of people from Santo Domingo (or people from Venezuela who were on the island) were actors in these relationships, and sometimes included Spanish soldiers fighting there.

"Caribe" (Caribbean) became code for a revolution to achieve colonial independence and the destruction of slavery and great landed estates—a nightmare for the slaveholding elites of Spanish America. At the same time, outside the area immediately affected, the revolution could be a great opportunity to accelerate export production on plantations worked by large numbers of slaves—an opportunity that was exploited especially by Cuba's elite. There the great estates were divided into smaller plots of land on which an efficient production of sugar and coffee could be pursued using slaves and techniques of organization that were at that time extremely modern. The Venezuelan oligarchies reacted politically with hysteria, and rejected any change, especially after 1804. In Venezuela, Cuba's example of modernizing export production was not followed. The elites feared more than anything a spread of Haiti's ideas and discourses to the majority of the pardos, not least because the men of this group constituted the majority of the militia. Among the pardos, a prosperous group known as *pardos benemeritos* had developed; they themselves owned slaves and were pressing for more political rights.[16]

This was the situation when Alexander von Humboldt was traveling in Venezuela (from August 1799 to the end of 1800). Humboldt had come to America as an enemy of the Jacobins and of slavery.[17] On the basis of his published works, an image of him has been constructed in which he decisively influenced the independence of the elites and of Simón Bolívar.[18] However, a reading of his research diaries from this time shows something quite different.[19] His discussions of "slaves" and "slavery" and his rejection of them are interwoven with the rejection of violent revolution as a political means.[20]

Both critical points are directed against two groups that, a mere decade later, were to spearhead the Creole independence movements of Spanish America: first, against the "generation of independence," young mantuanos who in Humboldt's time still clung to a kind of colonial autonomy (Andrés Ibarra, Francisco José de Caldas, Fernando Peñalver, the Ribas family, the Fernández de León brothers, and also Simón Bolívar and Francisco de Miranda, among others),[21] and second, against the pardos.[22] The Creoles rejected Humboldt, because they had become accustomed to colonial violence, advocated "French Terror," were racist, and harbored the wish to found a "white republic." Here we find combined Humboldt's two basic animosities, against slavery and against a "white republic" based on terror. Among the pardos, the matter was somewhat more complex.

Humboldt's own transculturality, with its Greco-Roman roots, reached its limit in his assessment of the pardos' "Afro-American" culture and their popular transformation of European values. However, that holds especially for his written judgments. In the pardos, Humboldt probably sensed the "mob" that could be a source of direct physical violence in a possible anticolonial rebellion. In Humboldt's personal relationship to the real world, there were hardly sharp boundaries.[23] Societies and ideas were in flux. In the whole Western world, debates about the cultural, individual, and ideal presuppositions for a "nation"[24] were then beginning. What Humboldt understood as "Jacobinism" between 1800 and 1805 is fundamental.[25]

In Europe in 1805, Jacobinism had a quite different meaning. For the Caribbean, which was experiencing the impact of the battles for the slave colony of Santo Domingo, Francisco de Arango y Parreño (1765–1837), a Cuban friend of Humboldt's,[26] best described what "Jacobinism" and "French Terror" meant at that historical moment. In 1803, Arango visited Santo Domingo (Cap Français), which was still held by French troops, in order to report to the Cuban hierarchies what the future might bring for Santo Domingo/Haiti and what effects on slavery in Cuba were foreseeable. In response to the rhetorical question: "¿qué suerte o destino tienen los negros que caen prisioneros?" (What fate or destiny awaits negroes who are taken prisoner?), the slaveholder and plantation owner Arango writes: "They all die, and that is how it has been since the last times of General Leclerc.[27] The easiest death for those unfortunates is to be shot or beaten to death, and it is still not the worst to be thrown into the sea, always bound back to back and always in pairs. What shocked me most came out of the mouth of the head of the brigade, Nerau, the commander of the guard of the commanding general, [who said] that in the preceding night he had thrown a captured negro to the dogs, and another [report says] that on that morning he had surprised a group of twelve rebels, whose leader was handed over to the [French] troops who had asked for him, so that they could tear out his eyes while he was still alive."[28]

For Arango and also for Humboldt, "Jacobinism" refers to the terror used by Jacobin French officers and soldiers against captured black and colored rebels who were fighting for freedom and equality. That is why in his still-unpublished diary for 1804, Humboldt laconically notes: "In 1803, terrorism reigns in the colonies."[29]

Humboldt's criticism of Fernando Peñalver (1765–1837)[30] is typical of his attitude toward Venezuela's colonial elites. While staying in Valencia, where the estate and slave holders had their summer houses, Humboldt said about Peñalver: "Don Fernando Peñalver, a cultivated man like his brother and just as skinny, but taller and considering himself an Adonis, wretchedly vain, in the first days speaking constantly about Raynal, the *Encyclopédie*, and human freedom. But later common human nature broke through. The Portuguese[31] said a white republic should be founded, at a time when the French republic has undoubtedly allowed slavery again[32] ...; in the white republic even the free mulattoes [pardos] are not given any rights, slaves serve their masters on their knees, and the masters sell the slaves' children.... That is the fruit of American Enlightenment! Banish your Encyclopedia and your Raynal, you infamous people."[33]

Seventeen years later, when it was a question of constituting the new state and determining the new power elites, Peñalver advised Simón Bolívar regarding the abolition of slavery and the granting of land. About Peñalver, Daniel F. O'Leary, who transmitted many details and anecdotes about Bolívar, says in his *Detached Recollections*, a kind of private notebook: "G[eneral] B[olivar].— Peñalver was considered one of his [Bolívar's] best friends and a fine man. It was also P[eñalver] who advised him to call a session of the congress in 1819. P[eñalver] was one of the few who used the familiar *tu* with G[eneral] B[olivar]."[34] Even if we interpret this passage cautiously, it clearly shows that Bolívar and Peñalver shared a number of basic convictions.

Humboldt was a supporter of the Bourbon (and also the Prussian) reformers. The Bourbon reforms definitely had a nation-building component and established a relatively centralized colony called Venezuela (1777–1810) with Caracas as its midpoint, but they had too little time, historically speaking, to be effective. This was not least a consequence of the Haitian revolution, the French Revolution, and the Napoleonic wars, which caused Atlantic relationships to break down completely (Trafalgar 1805). Everywhere wars, expulsions, land occupations, rebellions, and revolutions sprang up.[35] The cocoa bean industry had been in crisis since 1780.

The elites in Caracas concentrated more than ever on cattle raising in the Llanos. This led to serious conflicts and protracted border wars with the Llaneros from Apure. Units of the English fleet and corsairs cruised off Venezuela's coasts,[36] as was known even in distant Berlin.[37] This resulted in a great deal of work for the war ministry in Spain.[38] But Spain could no longer undertake much in America—the Atlantic connection had long been the Spanish Empire's Achilles' heel. Fearing a British conquest, in 1776 Madrid allowed French, Scottish, and Irish Catholics to settle on the island of Trinidad and to bring their slaves with them. The Britons took advantage of this option. They annexed the large island of Trinidad, then a province of the Captaincy General of Venezuela, with the support of the settlers and only five ships of the line.[39]

Since the beginning of the Caribbean crisis, the Dutch, Caribs, French, and Portuguese had been making even more inroads than before. Fugitive black slaves were establishing, as the Spaniards assumed, a "free and independent republic" in Essequibo and Surinam.[40] But in the center as well, in the cocoa bean region of Barlovento, slave settlements (*cumbes*) were emerging.[41] In the west, the English and smugglers from Jamaica and Nicaragua were delivering weapons to the Guajiro Indios.

The situation was dangerous and unstable. Since 1806, Creoles and Spaniards in America had been forced to settle their own affairs among themselves. In 1806, Francisco de Miranda (1750–1816), the son of a rich man from the Canary Islands who had been unable to make a career in Venezuela, tried to conquer Venezuela with the help of the United States. Starting with Venezuela, he planned a military expedition that was supposed to unite all of Spanish America in an enormous independent state. However, after succeeding in occupying Coro for a few days, the intruders had to withdraw for lack of support from the Venezuelan people and its elites.[42]

But the conflicts in the interior of Venezuela were much more extensive. The racial and caste barriers that the majority of the mestizos encountered became the greatest area of tension. The violence repressed in calmer times now flared up among social groups. Then in 1808 the Spanish homeland collapsed. Napoleon's troops occupied Madrid. Both Spanish kings, Charles IV and his unruly son Ferdinand VII, abdicated in favor of Napoleon's brother Joseph, who mounted the throne of the Bourbons in Madrid as José I. The majority of the reform elites in Spain were *afrancesados* who supported the French. On the other hand, provincial noblemen, military officers, priests, and farmers organized an extensive guerilla war against the French, though at first it was not successful. Local juntas emerged that repeatedly retreated to the south as the French advanced. Finally, on the Cádiz peninsula, sheltered by the cannons of the British navy, the anti-French forces had to surrender symbolic power over the rest of Spain and Spanish America to a regency council and at the same time convoke a parliament, the Cortes Generales. In the years preceding 1814, the Cortes carried out, especially with the constitution of 1812, the project of a Spain united in a "Nation on both sides of the Atlantic." The local elites in America, particularly on what had up to that point been the periphery of Venezuela and Rio de la Plata (Buenos Aires, Montevideo, Paraguay), subverted this project. In the confused two years between 1808 and 1810, the Spanish central junta called upon South American elites to vote in several elections. They also had to prevent the juntas in America from taking the ideas of autonomy too seriously and the Americans, who were more than twice as numerous as the European Spaniards, from constituting a majority in the parliament.

In Spanish America, the captains general and governors were under special pressure to solve these problems. After the mantuanos had made several attempts to create an independent junta of the Caracas elites in order to resolve the many local and regional difficulties and avoid a rebellion by the pardos, the Junta Conservadora de los Derechos de Fernando 7mo (Junta to preserve the rights of Ferdinand VII) was formed on April 19, 1810. The king's son, called *el deseado* ("the desired") was considered as a supporter of reform along the lines favored by the American elites. The Spanish captain general and the intendant were forced to resign. The mantuanos of Caracas thought that this "fortunate revolution" had ensured sovereignty. For them, in 1810 "the revolution in government" was ended. But the other cities were not ready to give up their independence and subject themselves to a government by elites from Caracas.[43]

The necessity of legitimating the new power opened the way for new forms of politics, sociability, journalism, and discourse. It goes without saying that this early phase of renewal was accompanied by hardly any myth. The elites of many of Venezuela's cities declared their autonomy and either followed Caracas's example or participated in the elections for the Cortes in Cádiz and thus backed the junta in Caracas. With the junta, the mantuanos of Caracas thought they could further develop their supremacy, which had now been strengthened by the first decrees on free trade. A constitutional convention, dominated by the Caracas elites and modeled on the North American model, was convened. However, the heated debates concerned the confederation and not, for example, the nation.[44]

Nonetheless, an interesting configuration emerged from the argument over general status as citizens. The convention in Caracas sought to speak on behalf of all the provinces of the general captaincy when it recognized the pardos as "people" with basic rights. In contrast, the delegates from the former provinces preferred to define the status of the pardos for their territories themselves, on the confederate model.[45] In any case, the confederate constitution of December 1811 emphasized, *expressis verbis*, the "limits of equality" for pardos. When the word "nation" was used, it was used in the sense of territory, but mainly only as *nación española* or *esta parte de la nación española* (this part of the Spanish nation—meaning Venezuela). This alluded to the whole Spanish Empire, from which they either expected more sovereignty or wanted to detach themselves.[46]

In July 1811, this dynamics of the new political culture led to the declaration of independence. A large part was played in this by the pressure exerted by the pardos and by radical young Creoles from the mantuano families of the generation born around 1780 gathered around Simón Bolívar and Francisco de Miranda, who had returned again to Caracas at the end of 1810.[47] For the nascent nineteenth century, the declaration of independence represented the true political revolution. New actors appeared in the public sphere, especially one usually designated as the *plebe* (people).[48] However, this was no longer the feudal "people," that is, the Spanish and Spanish American nobility and privileged classes, but rather all the strata of the country's population—with the exception of slaves and women.[49] After the outbreak of military conflicts at the end of 1810, the men of the country, and soon also slaves and former slaves, made their entrance on the political stage and took part in the battles for freedom and equality.

The Confederación Americana de Venezuela was founded by representatives from the Provincias Unidas of Caracas, Cumaná, Barcelona, Barinas, Margarita, Mérida, and Trujillo.[50] The proclamation of the new state, which did not even dare to call itself a republic, was a death sentence for the old elites that they themselves had formulated. Subsequently, a civil war broke out. At first, the mantuanos of Caracas had thought that with the traditional militias, now styled the "army," they could conquer the city of Coro, whose elites had refused to subject themselves to the convention in Caracas. The resulting dispute, which had been waged in words since the second half of 1810, expanded into an armed conflict.[51] Pardo militiamen rebelled against Caracas or deserted it. *Isleños* and Canary Islanders formed their own militias (*guerrillas*). Spurred on by Spanish officers, the slaves of Barlovento, Caracas's plantation zone, rebelled.[52] The church hierarchy opposed the republicanism of the Creole elites. When in March 1812 an earthquake destroyed large parts of Caracas, it was considered a divine punishment.[53]

The Bolívarianos, young Creole militia captains from Simón Bolívar's generation who moved to the center of the political stage in 1812/13, called themselves *patriotas* (patriots), but had not yet defined their "homeland." In colonial times, the most important area of membership was the *patria chica* (little homeland) of the city. It is true that there was neither any sense of community among the various population groups nor a national consciousness. Only a short-lived alliance between the elites of Caracas and officers of the pardo militias made possible the attempt to establish a republic in 1810.[54]

Subsequently, separate movements developed among the pardos, the Canary Islanders, the Llaneros, the slaves, the Bolívarianos, and groups from various parts of the country in the center and the east. Unusual alliances emerged that often fought with one another and put their own territorial ideas and views before the nation. Even small groups of intellectuals and international adventurers intervened in the conflicts. All these movements acted without Simón Bolívar, who since 1813 had played a certain role only among young militia officers. In 1815, Spain sent a large army to Venezuela, and many anti-Spanish leaders fled Venezuela and met in Haiti. In 1816, Bolívar also had to flee his place of exile in the English Caribbean (Jamaica) and asked President Alexandre Pétion (1770–1818) for help. Almost all of these men were liberal revolutionaries, and some were also republicans, spies, or adventurers. At this time, the Frenchman Jean-Nicolas Billaud-Varenne (1756–1819) and the Spanish guerilla leader Javier Mina (1789–1817)[55] met in Haiti on their way to Mexico.

Among the immigrants to Haiti—who were really a group of Creole militia officers in diaspora—were the mulatto officer Manuel Carlos Piar (1774–1817), the former military chief of eastern Venezuela after Bolívar had been discharged because of the defeat in 1814, and Santiago Mariño (1788–1854), Bolívar's old opponent from Cumaná. In addition there was a series of Creole militia officers: Pedro María Freites, Bartolomé Salom, Mariano Montilla,
José Antonio Anzoátegui, Bolívar himself, Pedro León Torres, José Francisco Bermúdez, Carlos Soublette, Pedro Briceño Méndez, Bolívar's long-time secretary, Manuel Valdés, Diego
Ibarra, the son of Vicente Ibarra and Ana Teresa Toro—Humboldt had mentioned the Ibarras by name in his criticism of the "white republic."

A group of radical liberals and internationalists was also present in Haiti: for instance, Gregor MacGregor (1786–1845), a Scottish adventurer and revolutionary who shortly afterward sought to found a "Republic of Florida";[56] the Polish emigrant Felipe Mauricio Martín (Filip Maurycy Marcinkowski, 1786–1853),[57] who fought on the British side at the battle of Trafalgar, participated in the Miranda expeditions, and was a Freemason; Pierre Villaume, alias Henri Ducoudray-Holstein (1763–1839),[58] an adventurer and Bolívar's (later) detractor[59] whom even Karl Marx read with pleasure;[60] and the botanist and politician Francisco Antonio Zea (1766–1822) from New Granada.

Among Mariño's comrades in arms were the colored captains and smugglers Juan Bautista Bideau (1780–1817)[61] and José Prudencio Padilla (1788–1828);[62] Luis Brión (1782–1821), a captain and later admiral of Great Colombia who was the son of a Walloon agent of the Obwexer textile firm in Augsburg (who had established a trading and smuggling network between Santo Domingo, Puerto Rico, Jamaica, Curaçao, and places on the Venezuelan coast);[63] the Acadian Renato Beluche (1773–1860), "the savior of New Orleans" (from the British in 1814);[64] and the British-Jamaican officer and adjutant William Carlos (Charles) Chamberlain (1790–1817)[65] as well as a series of pirates,[66] some of whom had escaped at the last minute the Spanish blockade around Cartagena.[67]

The most important sociopolitical movement within the militias, which called themselves armies or guerillas, was that of the pardos and mulattos, who had developed their own forms of republicanism "from below," but in some places—such as Valencia in Venezuela, because there the elites hoisted the banner of republicanism—they also fought under the banner of the monarchy. Their main goal was equality.[68] On the coasts of Venezuela, where the structure of slavery was limited in area but very dense, there were accordingly only very isolated slave rebellions, not the kind of massive resistance found in Santo Domingo/Haiti. Male slaves were repeatedly recruited in different ways, initially by Spanish officers who incited the slaves of Barlovento to rebel against the First Republic (1811/12).[69]

The largest and most powerful resistance movement was that of the Llaneros. The nation as a concept of the state was completely alien to them. Under José Tomás Boves (1782–1814), an Asturian sailor who had lived for a time as a cattle smuggler in the Venezuelan Llanos, the Llaneros swept away all the urban elite's attempts to form a state. They formed a temporary alliance with their enemies, that is, with Spanish priests and officers as well as with a few militias operating under leaders from the Canaries.[70] The militias of the *isleños* and poor whites collaborated very closely with Spanish officers, colonial officials, and royalist members of religious orders. For the most part, they were led by the proprietors of small shops or taverns, a sector (small business owners) dominated by the Canary Islanders and poor whites. Thus the militia officer Francisco Tomás Morales (1781–1844),[71] a "former seller of fried fish,"[72] and the Spanish clergyman José Ambrosio Llamozas advised the monarchist leader of the Llaneros. King Ferdinand VII was so shocked by the atrocities and the open way Llamozas described them in his report on the conduct of the war in the Llanos[73] that he refused to receive the priest.[74]

The bloody violence reached unanticipated proportions. According to Francisco Tomás Morales, Boves had under his command about 31,000 fighters, including many former slaves, free blacks, and pardos. In the Venezuelan context, where 1,000 soldiers were already considered a large number, this was the largest army of the nineteenth century.[75]

Not all movements pursued independence as their goal. A few groups sought improvements in their status, more rights, and a republican form of government, while others were primarily concerned with freedom and equality, and still others were intent on destroying their enemies (who were not always only Spaniards). In general, one of these movements of the waning republicanism "from below" that sought equality characterized the nineteenth century not only in Venezuela but in the former Spanish America as a whole, and constitutes one of the peculiar features of Latin America in the history of the Atlantic world.[76] The Bolívarianos, Bolívar's closest adherents and the executors of his legacy, fought on into the 1860s for a large state that would consist of at least New Granada and Venezuela. None of these movements succeeded completely, and none can be limited solely to the time between

1810 and 1821. The violence inherent in colonialism was unleashed in the chaotic battles among militias. There were no institutions, or only very rudimentary ones, to bring them under control again.

At best, this succeeded in the cities and provinces that were still allied with the Spanish Empire: Maracaibo until 1824, Coro until 1821, and Angostura until 1817. Starting from Coro and Maracaibo, where reinforcements from Cuba and Spain could be landed, the Spanish monarchy repeatedly regained power over the coasts. They did so first in 1812/13 under the Spanish captain Domingo de Monteverde (1773–1832) (who had been born in the Canary Islands), with the aid of a local guerilla leader, the Indio Juan de los Reyes Vargas, and many pardos and slaves. Under the Llanero leader Boves, these fresh attempts to form a state were completely smashed. However, the royalist units were a conglomeration of men who lived on war and threatened all the elites, including the Spanish ones. The great pacification of 1815, which took place under Pablo Morillo (1775–1837), who brought from Spain more than 11,000 veterans of the Napoleonic wars,[77] was therefore initially directed against the troops allied with Boves, who for their part had destroyed two attempts to establish stability under Bolívar (Caracas 1813/14) and Santiago Mariño (Cumaná 1813/14).

Representatives of the local elites in Venezuela, self-appointed patriots residing chiefly in Caracas and Cumaná, wanted to avert violence by establishing small states. But the latter were short-lived. In order to realize their republican goals, these patriots tried to direct aggression outward, against the Spaniards and the royalist Creoles. On this basis, nationalist historiography shaped the First Republic (1811/12), the Second Republic (1813/14), the Third Republic (1818/19), and so on. They are part of the Bolívar myth. None of these republics comprehended the whole area of Venezuela or amounted to more than an attempt to form a state. Caudillo systems, which spread in Venezuela after 1810, were more successful in controlling and directing violence.

The caudillo systems were extremely diverse.[78] As a rule, they operated under the leadership of a charismatic native who led the intrepid and skilled militias, whose leaders were bound to him by kinship or quasi-kinship. Caudillos remained as supreme leaders so long as they were successful and provided their troops with benefits. In the territories they controlled, caudillos both used violence and represented it.[79] They often formed alliances with the caudillos of territories bordering their own, especially when one of those leaders had better access to weapons and commodities. Thus caudillo pyramids emerged in which the subordinate leaders stood in some kinship relationship to the supreme leader. A culture of violence is characteristic of the caudillo system. As Maríano Picón Salas described (later) caudillos: "They all had been thrashed in virile battles against the Republic's regulars, but they were persistent and capable of eating the worst *laib casabe* [bread made of yucca meal] and drinking bad water from a puddle on the *llanos*. They knew their men personally and had trained their own officers."[80]

In Venezuela, the Llanero movement, which had turned away from the Spaniards in 1815 and allied itself with militias under Bolívar, produced a caudillo who ended up being elected in 1831 as the first president of the republic: José Antonio Páez (1790–1873). All the main leaders of Venezuela's civil wars between 1810 and 1824, and indeed in the nineteenth century as a whole, were also caudillos.[81] Between 1816 and 1818, Simón Bolívar himself seemed to be a more martial caudillo. In any case, he still enjoyed legitimacy and relations with militia officers from the old urban elites, out of which he constantly strove to make an army on the European model. He secured legal recognition not only through naked force but also through the support of authorities (such as England or the presidents of other countries) or through elections held by officers' councils (the Llaneros also practiced these "council" elections). This legitimation preceded the one he was able to gain through liberal congresses or constitutions at a later stage in Independencia and with which he was able to establish himself institutionally over other leaders.

Bolívar also underpinned his movement by means of a nationalist discourse of violence. In May 1813, he had a declaration of *guerra a muerte* (war to the death) issued, printed up, and distributed.[82] In reality, terror had been raging since the end of 1810, when armed conflict began. Precisely what Bolívar intended to achieve with this declaration regarding the channeling of violence remains a subject of debate. Presumably it was to justify the motto (known not only in Venezuela) "The most radical man should be the leader," or to check counterviolence in order to keep the atrocities of civil war at least somewhat under control. At a minimum, the printed word emphasized his claim to leadership. And it shows that Bolívar was a capable and realistic leader.

The *guerra a muerte* established with a specific discourse two national camps: "Spaniards and Canary Islanders, if you do not actively help Venezuela win its freedom you must reckon with death, even if you are only undecided. Americanos, you must reckon with life, even if you are guilty."[83] By Americanos, Bolívar meant all "good people" of the continental society, all who had been born in America, even if they stood on the king's side. Spaniards and Canary Islanders could save themselves from death only if they fought actively for an America freed from Spain alongside the patriots gathered around Bolívar. The decree provided the ideal construction of a continental nation that in reality did not exist at all.[84] In general terms, the militia officers around Simón Bolívar and a few allied Bolívarianos resorted to caudillismo and terror, as Humboldt predicted, in order to channel the violence unleashed and make use of it for their purposes. They had competitors. Above all, Bolívar succeeded first in drawing the most important patriotic leader of the pardos, Manuel Piar, over to his side (1816), and then excluding him (1817). To do so, Bolívar even had to draw on elements of social revolution: male slaves who had fought in the army were set free and granted land in the form of certificates of authorization (*vales*). By betraying Piar, in 1817 Bolívar and his troops were able to occupy rich missionary areas belonging to the Capuchin monks and the region around the city of Angostura, which reached, via the mouth of the Orinoco, as far as the Atlantic and the Caribbean and thus attracted smugglers and pirates who allied themselves with the new holders of power.

The life histories of these smugglers can be very interesting. For example, John Alderson (1785–1846) had come to Caracas from the island of Trinidad in 1811. He joined the patriots. Under the royalist Monteverde, Alderson was imprisoned for a short time, but was set free through the intervention of the British admiral John Durham. When the patriots' cause seemed lost, Alderson tried his chance in royalist Caracas and set up, together with the Basque businessman José Toribio, a firm that engaged in wholesale flour trade between Baltimore and Caracas. Wheat flour was the basis of the upper classes' diet; the lower strata of society ate yucca and corn flour. Alderson was also involved in financial transactions (*letras de cambio*) between London and Venezuela. In 1817/18, he moved his business back to Angostura, under patriotic protection. He smuggled weapons, munitions, and food and handled the transportation of European soldiers to Venezuela. Bolívar and Alderson formed a "firm friendship." When the Bolívarian troops invaded, Alderson reestablished his business in Caracas. The Alderson family had belonged to Caracas's upper stratum since 1824, according to his naturalization document (*carta de naturalización*). His eldest daughter, Elizabeth (Isabel) Alderson, later became the first woman to publish a literary review in Venezuela (*Ensayo Literario*, 1872/73). At first, Alderson leased run-down haciendas from impoverished mantuano families, for example, the Hacienda Bello Monte, which had earlier belonged to the Ibarra family (Humboldt and the French naturalist Bonpland often stayed there; today, it is a part of Caracas). When the family could not repay loans, Alderson took full possession of the hacienda. He was also the leaseholder of José Antonio Páez's famous Hacienda La Trinidad. Thus it was no wonder that Alderson was involved in the rebellion that led in 1830 to the separation of Venezuela from Great Colombia. Later on, he belonged to the most conservative groups of the so-called *hacendados* who supported José Antonio Páez's regime. Alderson subsequently worked on the project to found a Banco Mercantil de Descuento y Depósito (Mercantile Discount and Deposit Bank) in Caracas and took an active part in the debates about the right to vote.[85]

Back to the year 1818: in Angostura, an army had been formed by massive hiring of European veterans who had just ended their service in the Napoleonic wars, a fresh attempt to organize a state had been made, and another congress convened (Congreso de Angostura). In spite of all this, Bolívar and his army composed of Creole militias, forcibly recruited soldiers, and European soldiers were unable to integrate the caudillos into his concept of a Napoleonic strategy. In 1819, he had to leave Venezuela with his selected troops and cross the Andes to Bogotá (in the resource-rich region of Cundinamarca). Nationalist historiography has presented this passage over the Andes as a heroic, triumphal march. In fact, it was a desperate maneuver. But because of the unexpected successes in Bogotá, the Bolívarian movement now had an abundance of resources. The state of Colombia, today called Great Colombia to distinguish it from the state then called New Granada, emerged in 1819 and existed until 1830. It was another attempt at stabilization as a smaller variant on Miranda's large continental state. Only then did people begin to refer to those who came from the former colonial subareas of this state (to use modern names, Panama, New Granada, Venezuela, and Ecuador) as Venezuelans, New Grenadans, and Ecuadorians. Basically, except for military actions in 1821 and 1827, Bolívar never returned to Venezuela but instead devoted himself to the continental war against armies under Spanish leadership.

In Venezuela, the dissolution of colonial rule was reflected institutionally and socially in the constitution, liberal newspapers, and public discussions. In practice, the surviving urban elites allowed themselves to be militarily liberated by the Bolívarian troops, in which the colored Llanero cavalry under Páez played the leading role. Directly after the victory of the *libertadores*, they reestablished the old order: the estate economy (hacienda, *hato*), slavery (*ley de manumisión*, 1821), and the criminal law regarding the protection of private property. There was a "slave punishment" for "disturbing the public order and attacks on property": public whipping.[86]

Landed estates and slaves were privatized, that is, they became full property in the sense of the Roman law tradition, and the forms of violence prevalent in the colonial tradition continued. The reconstruction of previous relationships concerning the ownership of large tracts of land is particularly clear; in relation to slavery, it is less clear. Basically, the congresses of Angostura (1819) and Cúcuta (1821) endorsed the recognition of slavery and the current status of each slave, male or female. This meant, first of all, that former slaves who were in the army remained free, and the rest remained in their place of work. With the *ley de manumisión*, the concept of *esclavitud* (slavery) was replaced by that of manumission (i.e., legal emancipation), and slavery merely masked. All children born after 1821 were to be free in accord with the "law of the free womb,"[87] but to remain with their mothers and their masters. Slave trading remained forbidden, though masters were allowed to take "servants" (i.e., former slaves) with them, and these were often sold as slaves abroad—for example, in Cuba. Both male and female slaves could be freed in exchange for compensation or their freedom bought by special commissions. This was written into the constitution of Cúcuta (1821)—one of the world's most mendacious "freedom laws." It ensured that slave owners could retain their "invested capital" for at least a generation and left abolition under the control of the government (in which the slaveholders set the tone). Slavery was ultimately not abolished in Venezuela until 1854.[88]

The surviving elites, along with a few officers who had risen in society, also set in motion, with the help of the state, a gigantic process of accumulation. By means of rapid privatization and the sale of all common property (ecclesiastical property, Indio village communities, the land of "free" Indios in the south and in the Guyanas, the allocation of private property in the Llanos, and the appropriation of herds), more and more land came under their control. All this was propagated in the language of liberalism (especially with reference to Jeremy Bentham) and surrounded with a few liberal measures (e.g., the abolition of the poll tax for Indios). Because of their military successes, a few high-ranking officers in the Bolivarian army had to be accepted into the new landed-estate elites, even if they were dark pardos. José Antonio Páez became one of the largest landowners. In spite of that fact or precisely because of it, even someone like Bolívar never lost his fear of the pardos.[89] Caudillo types who knew the rough speech of the Llaneros became politicians. Apart from short-term exceptions, no member of the white elites managed any longer to become president of Venezuela. The caudillos' culture of violence and the memory of the massacre of the old urban elites in the civil wars between 1810 and 1821 weighed too heavily. Nevertheless, the structures of control over land and the labor force were retained and further developed, now as capitalist property and export goods for the Atlantic market. Thus a kind of independence revolution that retained slavery and colonial landownership had come into the world. In every generation, however, caudillos found it easy to mobilize again the sons of slave women and peons (indentured servants) against landowners and the governments that represented them. For that reason, politicians in Venezuela even today have to be capable of communicating with a rebellious rural population and its descendants in the barrios, have to know their language and the macho rituals of caudillismo.

In direct connection with Humboldt's work that was appearing just then (1812–1824), the elites began, especially in Caracas, to construct the myth of "the" Independencia, that is, a single Independencia led by elite Creoles like Simón Bolívar and owed nothing to other movements. A closed spatiotemporal complex was invented that gives the impression that from 1810 to 1821, every resident of the Venezuela colony rose up against the Spanish, under the leadership of the Creoles. Starting with the Caracas revolution of April 19, 1810, the myth included several republics designated by Roman numerals, on the model of the French Revolution from 1789 to 1795. Humboldt's work, especially his *Relation historique*,[90] which is basically a long commentary on the history of Venezuela, was a major source of legitimacy, because Humboldt wrote his diaries while traveling—in real time, so to speak—from 1799 to 1804. However, he published them only after a phase of reworking them (1812–1826) in which he suppressed many direct judgments and commented cautiously on the new context that had emerged after his stay in Venezuela. In this, he was realistic enough to recognize that among the many movements, at least that of the

Bolívarianos was a kind of Creole-liberal revolution (1810–1821). This allowed the surviving mantuanos and their intellectuals to appeal to Humboldt after 1821. Thus they saw themselves as the originators of this Creole-liberal revolution, although after the earthquake and the defeats of 1812, they had in fact abandoned any idea of a rebellion. For almost seven years (1815–1821), the mantuanos supported the restoration regime under General Pablo Morillo against Bolívar and against the other movements as well.[91]

Caudillos and Bolívar Revenants: Nineteenth-Century Experiments with the State

Against this background, the history of the two centuries that followed can be quickly recounted. The liberation by the Bolívarian army and the attempt to establish a state on the liberal model quickly led to a seizure of power by the most powerful old oligarchies in Venezuela. Between 1826 and 1830, the oligarchies, with the help of the caudillo Páez, destroyed the Bolívarian experiment of Great Colombia.

The reason for this was the recruitment of their slaves by Bolívar's army, which had just "liberated" Peru and feared an intervention by the Holy Alliance. Only then were the state and the nation, which were still essentially seen as identical, founded with the forename Venezuela—"The Venezuelan Nation." At first this occurred only in words; it did not have actual consequences for state institutions, territorial sovereignty, legislation, citizenship, or fiscal authority everywhere. The conservatives, then called *godos* (Goths), founded the Fourth Republic of Venezuela in 1830, under President Páez. Based on a successful coffee and cattle exporting economy, it remained stable until the great crisis of Atlantic agrarian economies (1842/43).

Anyone who sees Independencia historically as a temporally and spatially delimited unity that ended in 1821 or 1830, overlooks one thing: The Pandora's box opened by the beginning of military conflicts could not be closed again before the end of the "bloody nineteenth century." The situation remained fundamentally very

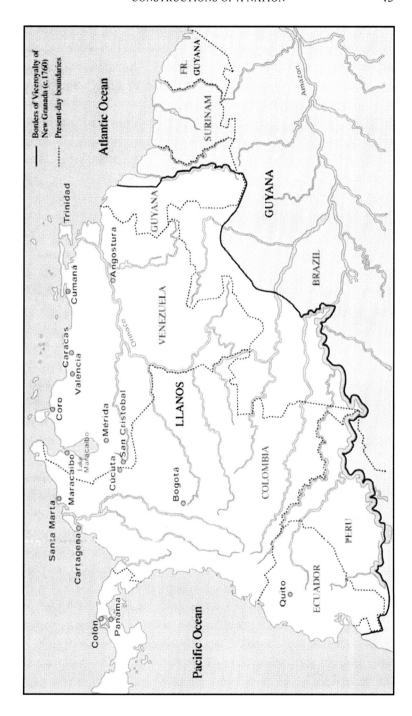

unstable, especially with the experimentation going on. That was shown not only by the many autonomy accords that were negotiated among elites in the center, the east, and the west, such as the Revolución de las Reformas in 1835/36. It was also visible in the various conceptions of space, in which Venezuela on maps and in the provinces controlled by caudillos seemed more real than it did as a nation-state. It was expressed in the many changes affecting the size of the provinces, their names, and their capital cities. And it appeared in the border conflicts between the newly emerged states and the violent attacks made by other powers (such as Great Britain's in Guyana). Both government bodies and economic and social factors were characterized by extreme instability, and this was reflected in discourses. Combative rebels, sometimes under prominent caudillos and sometimes under unknown and nameless leaders, competed with statesmen and state powers or with big landowners and their private militias.

In 1846, the caudillo dynasty of the Monagas rose up out of eastern Venezuela (the *oriente*) in the wake of great agrarian and trade crises (1842/43 and 1847). In interaction with new peasant uprisings and caudillo systems, these violent conflicts finally amounted to a major war. In the *guerra de la federación* (1859–1864) the noncentral liberal elites, even though they were often led by young, power-hungry men from Caracas, won out over the central conservative elites under the old José Antonio Páez. Whereas this conflict, the most severe of all in the history of nineteenth-century Venezuela, the general of the liberals, Ezequiel Zamora[92] (1817– 1864), a peasant leader who was an intellectual and a former cattle smuggler who was familiar with both the language of the peons and the ideas of utopian socialism, took over almost complete power in the country and introduced an agrarian revolution. But he was shot from behind by his own men.

People now talked about *nación* in the sense of the different camps: the federal liberals, who had endorsed some of the demands of the peasants, constituted the *nación liberal* (known as "the Yellows") versus the conservative nation of the oligarchs (nicknamed "the Blues").

Because of these conflicts, Venezuela was often threatened by external interventions, especially after 1850, when gold was found in Guyana (the Essequibo conflict with Great Britain). The state territory, explored by costly expeditions and outlined in prestigious atlases, steadily shrank—particularly in the west, in the Llanos and the La Goajira peninsula (now a borderland between Colombia and Venezuela), and in the south, where the enormous Roraima (Rio Branco) region was transferred to Brazil.

After nearly eighty years of uprisings, revolutions, and caudillo wars, the regime headed by Juan Vicente Gómez (1857–1935) began in 1908 and lasted almost thirty years. This was a "liberal" dictatorship, but it maintained free trade and after 1920 used oil exports to pay off Venezuela's enormous debts. These were old debts dating from the period of Independencia and the conservative stabilization, as well as new debts incurred during the phase of liberal modernization (1870–1888) under Antonio Guzmán Blanco, which had presented itself as a "civilizing autocracy" on the French model.[93] A period of rapid economic expansion in Venezuela began. At the same time, Guzmán Blanco succeeded in controlling caudilloism and republicanism "from below." Large reserves of oil were discovered and lent impetus to the search for natural resources in the enormous territory. Moreover, a process of "Caracasization" began—a still stronger centralization under the cloak of federalism. However, the bill was financed in advance by means of loans made by foreign sources.[94]

Now politicians and the press definitely began to talk about the nation. The elites already saw Venezuela as the "France of the South."[95] However, they were even more eager to be transferred to diplomatic posts in Europe. In reality, the elites, who still defined themselves as white, claimed to have nothing in common with the colored peasants. Slavery was abolished in 1854, when the slaves were so old that they could no longer be exploited.[96]

The Conservative and Revolutionary Bolívar in the "Age of Extremes"

In 1908, a new period of dictatorships, putsches, and popular uprisings began, at the dawn of the twentieth century as the "Age of Extremes" (Eric Hobsbawm). Under the liberal Gómez dictatorship, Venezuela underwent an economic boom and a reorientation. The system of landed estates was retained as a sort of status symbol, but starting in the 1920s, Venezuela relied increasingly on the production and export of oil. The haciendas became partly areas for oil-prospecting, capitalistic agrarian industries, or objects of speculation for urban construction. A few haciendas near cities, especially in Caracas, were turned into parks and clubs for the new urban upper classes.

The lack of agrarian reform drove the peasants off the land. Because they hoped to find greater earning opportunities in the cities and in the oil industry, they went to live in the barrios. The result was a massive wave of migration within the country and immigration from Iberian countries and from Colombia. Until about 1928, the population of the country, which is as large as France and Germany combined, continued to hover around three million. But after 1928, the population exploded in cities and immigration increased. Modern Venezuela emerged. The great majority of people were nonetheless still peasants in their mentality and extremely poor. Surplus oil revenues were used to pay off debts, to compensate for the financial crisis of 1929 and—especially after 1936—to finance a series of social projects such as schools and clinics. Under the dictatorship, a modern army emerged as the soul of the new nation. This army was controlled and led by the last caudillo, Juan Vicente Gómez, who had at the same time dealt the coup de grace to the old caudilloism. Ever since, in the discourse, the army had been very closely connected with the concept of the nation. However, most of the army still consisted of the dark-haired men who served as soldiers and subordinate officers, whereas in the nineteenth century, the middle class that had emerged along with the oil once again defined itself as white and was fixated on other countries, first on England, then on France, then on Germany, and after 1902, chiefly on the USA.

The myth of a conservative Simón Bolívar increasingly emerged as the heart of this nationalist discourse. The construction of a conservative foundational myth as a civil-religious legitimation had already begun in 1844, under Páez's presidency. And this happened even though Bolívar, who was still alive in 1830, had been declared persona non grata under Páez as well. Páez and his advisors integrated a godlike Bolívar into the myth of the single, self-enclosed Independencia that had been created as early as 1821. The cult of the nation around Simón Bolívar led, on the one hand, to the bookshelves of Venezuelan history being full of archives (writings, letters, edicts, decrees, speeches, memoirs) by and relating to the Liberator and the Bolívarianos that have preserved all of Bolívar's statements. On the other hand, since 1870, Venezuela's power elite has seen to it that the walls of national institutions are provided with artistic representations of heroes and battles. Nearly every picture that today illustrates works on Independencia is therefore a visual invention that was produced after 1870.[97]

This new form of nationalist discourse goes back to positivism. A series of positivist intellectuals—for example, the brilliant sociologist Laureano Vallenilla Lanz (1870–1936)—publicly declared their support for Gómez's stabilizing dictatorship. In his work on "the necessary policeman" (*gendarme necesario*), Vallenilla Lanz emphasized above all the role of (military) force, symbolized by an individual person, as the power of order versus the chaos of races, civil wars, passions, and landscapes. Thus his independent analysis of Venezuelan history provided, first of all, a historical and sociological legitimation for the dictator Gómez. Second and more important, he created, if not the fundamental type of Bolívar interpretation, then at least its basis: the problem of unbridled violence (to use Humboldt's term, "terror"). To do so, Vallenilla Lanz drew not only on the old Bolívar myth of the nineteenth century but also on the widespread admiration for José Antonio Páez (and the stories about him). He thus coined the notion of *Cesarismo democratico* (democratic Caesarism),[98] what was ultimately a sociological-positivistic definition of precisely the legend that there had been one and only one Independencia with only one leader, and that it was victorious because only the Liberator could control the violence.

The age of peasant insurrections led by caudillos came to a definitive end under Gómez's dictatorship. The remaining anti-oligarchical Llaneros, who were chronically hostile to the government, had retreated further into the depths of the Orinoco plains (where they were found in the 1920s by the writer Rómulo Gallegos while he was working on his novel *Doña Bárbara*[99]).

The first major conflicts based on a new political culture broke out in 1928: students symbolically clad in workers' clothing and berets used urban forms of protest.[100] When Gómez finally died in 1935, new, chiefly leftist organizations and parties emerged in which students, workers, and labor unions played an important role. Soon the rather nationalist and more influential Acción Democrática (AD), emerged that combined, under Rómulo Betancourt, Stalinism and an atavistic caudilloism, along with a trans-Caribbean internationalist Communist Party more strongly oriented toward the Communist International. From 1936 to 1941, conservative military men using violence, pressure, and oil-financed social measures saw to it that these new political actors were unable to establish themselves. A breakup of Gomezism, which would have had to include land reform and a reorganization of the oil industry, was avoided.

During his presidency (1941–1945), the left-liberal military officer Medina Angarita attempted to implement all these, but he was overthrown in the so-called October Revolution by an alliance of young military officers and the AD. The man of letters Rómulo Gallegos then became president, and a debate about the "resources of the nation" began: the nation was conceived as a body that had so many resources (oil, coal, and other raw materials) that every Venezuelan could be prosperous—but the state had to ensure, by redistribution, that the wealth of the nation could benefit everyone.[101] Leftist intellectuals also sought to redefine Bolívarism. Although they made very substantial contributions to historiography, they ran up against two barriers: the leaden power of conservative positivism, especially in the form of the "necessary policeman" (Vallenilla Lanz) and Marx's article "Bolivar y Ponte," which had been circulating in Latin America since 1936.[102] Marxists and their fundamental recognition that revolutions were the means of changing society—a view that Vallenilla Lanz had shared—soon came to be called "Marxistas-Vallenistas."

Thus the debate about the nation and the state turned, even during additional putsches (military coup, 1948) and a new dictatorship (Marcos P. Jiménez, 1952–1958), around a conservative Bolívar cult that since the 1980s has diversified into a "green Bolívar," a "women's Bolívar," and even a "lifestyle Bolívar." Nor was this changed by the so-called Punto Fijo democracy (1959–1999) and the serious financial and economic crisis it endured. That was logical insofar as the Punto Fijo democracy was based on a pact negotiated to oppose both the radical left, which had played the leading role in the popular uprising against the Jiménez dictatorship, and Fidel Castro. This conservative Bolívar myth and cult were, however, always counteracted by the popular imagination's social-revolutionary and at the same time esoteric-magical Bolívar. The cult of this Bolívar interprets the history of the country (and the nation) in its own way. The latter is given material form, for instance, in the dark-haired Bolívar images of Venezuela's transcultural María Lionza religion.

CHAPTER II

Simón Bolívar: The Man and the Myth

The Glorious Bolívar Family

A person's individual development begins in his family, and especially with his mother and father. At the time of the wedding of Simón Bolívar's parents in 1773, more than a few rumors were circulating among their contemporaries, because Juan Vicente Bolívar y Ponte (1726–1786) was thirty-two years older than his bride, María de la Concepción Palacios y Blanco (1758–1792).[1] The wealthy forty-six-year-old Creole[2] was engaged to marry a fourteen-year-old girl. At that point, the future father of Simón Bolívar was an old bachelor, the former *procurador* of the *ayuntamiento* of Caracas (1747), a high-ranking militia officer, and a *justicia mayor* (local judge), while María de la Concepción, who descended from the powerful Palacios family, was an adolescent beauty. According to the rule of the *quince* (the celebration of a girl's fifteenth birthday, which in Latin America still marks a kind of puberty rite), she could be married by her family.[3]

Thus girls with this social standing were sought after by older men who wanted to form alliances with powerful families. Before his marriage, Don Juan Vicente Bolívar had already shown his preference for very young women.[4] In one document in the archbishopric, a girl even describes him as a *lobo infernal* (hellish wolf).[5]

In any case, María de la Concepción gave birth to five children: the eldest son, Juan Vicente (1781–1811), the heir to the family *mayorazgos* (i.e., most of the inheritance remained undivided and inalienable); a second son, Simón; daughters María Antonia (1777–

1842) and Juana (1779–1847); and a third daughter born after her father's death who died in infancy.

The four siblings were orphaned at a very young age. Simón was three years old when his father died, and nine when his mother died.[6] From the outset, Simón Bolívar was surrounded by imaginary stories and old wives' tales. It was a difficult and, because of the family's social status, admired childhood. For an anthropologically oriented social history, a glance at the most important members of the family is very informative. Because of his early loss of his parents, these stories told by relatives and contemporaries may have played a major and compensatory role in Bolívar's development. At bottom, they had one thing in common: *gloria* (fame or glory). The most important Venezuelan critic of the Bolívar myth, Germán Carrera Damas, wrote: "Bolívar was obsessed by the desire for glory; it was a constant tendency of his personality, the ever-present vector of his historical actions."[7]

But glory was not everything. Like his father and the male portion of the mantuano oligarchy, Simón Bolívar also carried on a very active love and sex life: we know of seventeen women who were his lovers. Moreover, he lived for a long time with Manuelita Sáenz, the wife of a wealthy English merchant named Dr. Thorne.[8]

A turbulent life and the striving for glory required a firm foundation. This was manifested still more in the social standing of the family-clan of the Palacios and Bolívars than solely in the individual development of Simóncito, as Simón was called as a child. The *narratio* of his childhood and youth constitutes the soul of the myth as reflected, for instance, in the constantly recurring reference to his upbringing by Simón Rodríguez, who introduced him to the works of French Enlightenment thinkers (e.g., Rousseau's *Émile*) or the "encounter with Humboldt" in 1804.

A brief aside concerning the two *apellidos* (family names) is worthwhile. They show how closely Simón Bolívar was interconnected with the oldest and most power families in the oligarchy of Caracas and Spanish America. In Castilian culture, every legitimate child has two surnames—a paternal *apellido* as the first surname (the father's first *apellido*) and a maternal *apellido* as the second surname (the mother's first *apellido*). Simón Bolívar's[9] complete name is thus Simón Bolívar y Palacios, composed of the *apellidos* of his parents, Juan Vicente Bolívar y Ponte and María de la Concepción Palacios y Blanco, as the "masculine" and "feminine" surnames. His mother's family was more prominent and its members cared for Simóncito when he became an orphan, since the uncles and aunts on his father's side were very elderly. His maternal uncle Esteban Palacios Blanco, who had gone to Cádiz in 1792, made preparations for Simón's arrival in Spain in 1799, where he was to complete his education.[10]

Simón Bolívar was born into an elite family to which the idea of revolution was totally alien. Most studies mention the fact that the future Liberator's family was prominent and long established, but it has scarcely been described in accord with the rules of an anthropological social history and life history. It is still more difficult to determine the precise facts concerning the Bolívar family clan's ownership of property and slaves.

In Search of the Ancestors

Basques were involved in Spain's colonial expansion almost from the beginning, because in the Basque country almost everyone belonged to the *hidalguía universal*, a kind of general low nobility. That also held for the ancestor for whom Simón Bolívar (1783–1830) was named, the original Simón de Bolívar (1532–1612). After long service in Santo Domingo, the latter arrived in Caracas, which had been founded in 1567, where he became an important member of the royal administration (*procurador general, regidor perpetuo*)—not least because of his Basque *hidalguía*. The title of *procurador general* was given to the members of the local *cabildo* (municipal council) who represented the interests of this council and the city in dealings with the Crown. From 1590 to 1592, Bolívar the elder was in Spain. He acquitted himself well—especially in the interest of the *conquistador* elite of the city. Caracas was granted the title of *ciudad* as well as a royal coat of arms, which made it a full-fledged *villa* with all the associated rights. More than that: Bolívar the elder also succeeded in getting the prohibition on the *encomienda* lifted, which allowed the city to force Indios to work. In addition, he received the *licencia* to bring three thousand slaves directly from Africa to Caracas and to sell part of these slaves outside the city as well.

One might even go so far as to say that Bolívar the elder, who was also known to his contemporaries as "Simón the Basque" or Simón the *procurador*, was among the founders of slavery and the oppression of the Indios, African slaves, and other underclasses in Venezuela. In 1593, the governor gave him the title of *contador general de la Real Hacienda* (royal customs officer). The Bolívar family also received a side chapel in the Caracas cathedral.

Bolívar the elder thus was counted among the new regional colonial elite that arose after the phase of the Welser concession. Venezuela's peripheral areas had succeeded in attracting the attention of the Spanish Crown fundamentally only because they bordered on Portuguese possessions and especially, at the end of the sixteenth century, because they had to be secured against the advances of the English (Walter Raleigh) and Dutch (salt fleets sent to Araya). The Welser episode (1528–1556) did not shape Venezuela's social history,[11] but it did leave clear traces[12] in the family history of the Bolívars. On her mother's side, Simón's mother, María de la Concepción Palacios y Blanco, descended from a family clan with the name of Xedler (Gedler or Schedler)—no doubt a name from southern Germany.[13] However, more important for understanding the person of Simón Bolívar are his connections with "Simón the Basque" and his side of the family.

Bolívar's family ancestry conceals a few secrets. In the sixteenth century, one of the Blancos married a woman with the Flemish name of Gerardt and then emigrated to the Indies.[14] Among the Liberator's female ancestors, at the beginning of the eighteenth century, was María Petronila de Ponte, the second wife of his great-great grandfather, Juan de Bolívar. Her mother was the illegitimate child of a woman who was entered in the baptismal register only by her first names, María Josefa—and this usually indicated descent from a connection between a master and female slave.[15] In the popular version of the Bolívar myth, this was the starting point for pardo (mulatto) Bolívar.[16] The pardo caste represented about 50 percent of the population in the eighteenth-century colonial census and was thus the largest social group in Venezuela.

In 1802, during his first sojourn in Europe (1700–1802), Bolívar married the daughter of the related Toro clan, María Teresa del Toro y Alayza (1781–1803), who died of yellow fever only a year later. It was a type of marriage among relatives that was common in these circles. It deviated from normal elite behavior only because it was probably truly a love match. Bolívar was younger than his wife. But the marriage was considered successful by the oligarchies because it made possible the connection of the wealth and possessions of the two clans—the Toros and the Bolívars.

A direct marriage between relatives occurred when Simón Bolívar's sister, Juana Bolívar y Palacios, married her maternal uncle, Dionisio Palacios y Blanco. Their two children, Guillermo and Benigna Palacios y Bolívar, produced the only children in the nuclear Bolívar family who still have living descendants today.

The Bolívars' Fortune

As in every slave-holding family, two slave women cared for the little Simón Bolívar from his birth. The first was his nurse, Hipólita (c. 1763–1835), a slave from the Hacienda El Ingenio on the Mayorazgo San Mateo who was married to the slave Mateo, also part of the Bolívar's property. After she was set free in 1821, she used the last name Bolívar (corresponding to the first *apellido* of one of her last owners). Later on, young Simón was cared for by the *aya* (housekeeper) Matea (1773–1886;), who had been born on a *hato* near San José de Tiznados (Guarico).[17]

When he was still a very young man, Simón Bolívar, without having lifted a finger, came into the possession of five great legacies: in 1795 he inherited, at the innocent age of twelve or thirteen, the Mayorazgo de la Concepción, the legacy of his deceased first cousin, Presbitero Dr. Juan Félix de Aristiguieta y Bolívar.[18] This cousin was the eldest son of his aunt Petronila Bolívar y Ponte, his father's sister. She had married a man from the powerful Aristiguieta clan, Miguel Jérez de Aristiguieta Lovera. Partly because it produced many daughters, this was one of the largest and most influential families of the land-owning aristocracy of Caracas.[19]

Aunt Petronila died relatively early, and her widowed husband married again. With his second wife, Josefa Blanco Herrera, he produced nine daughters, whom Venezuelan historians call *las nueve musas* (the nine muses). In Caracas, between 1783 and 1790, young women who came from the most important family clans, were between fifteen and thirty years of age, and were looking for a husband with a suitable social status (a few were already married) were all called *las Aristiguieta*. They maintained close relationships with the six daughters of the Palacios y Blanco clan, to which the mother of Simón Bolívar also belonged.

Governor Manuel González Torres de Navarra had had Caracas's first coliseum built. The Escuela de Música de Chacao laid the foundations for the Venezuelan fascination with classical music, which was then not "classical" but simply fashionable among the elites, and was also spread by the visits to Caracas made by French aristocrats (Prince de Broglie, the Count of Ségur, Louis Alexandre Berthier, et al.). This founded the myth of Bolívar as the lover of "Western" musical high culture. Many of the costumbrist myths surrounding the Bolívar family arose from stories about this time.

As a younger son, Bolívar did not receive from the paternal heritage the family's most important *mayorazgo*, San Mateo, but at first only a smaller share of the heritage than his firstborn brother. *Mayorazgo* is a concept in Spanish law that prohibits the breaking up of a large estate through distribution to multiple heirs. Not until 1811, when his brother Juan Vicente was killed in a shipwreck while bringing in weapons for the Caracas junta, did Simón receive the whole family inheritance, including the copper mines in the Aroa valley.[20] From his mother, Simón inherited a few haciendas. And he received a fourth inheritance from the estate of his maternal grandfather, the *regidor* and *alférez real* Feliciano Palacios. In 1813, when he began his political career as the leader of the independence movement, Simón Bolívar was, by both contemporary and modern standards, a very rich man. One part of his first inheritance, the Mayorazgo de la Concepción, included about sixty-five male and female slaves. And individually, each of the later inheritances could have been the basis for the status of a very wealthy aristocrat.[21] Bolívar remained essentially in this position to the end of his life, even when he no longer personally administered his estates and left their management to his family. He would have liked to sell part of his possessions to finance his political activity.

Fundamentally, Bolívar never detached himself from the habitus of his class—he thought, dressed, tasted, smelled, and spoke like it, possibly in a somewhat more elevated way or using the language of Atlantic liberalism. In any case, after 1808 and especially after his sojourn in Haiti in 1816, his behavior and certainly his relationships were no longer those of a member of the land- and slave-holding elite. He no longer directly exploited slaves or had any immediate interest in his landholdings—that was true for him personally and also in his public role as Liberator, but not for his family and certainly not for the other representatives of the old (and new) oligarchies. Bolívar himself may have sensed this cleavage when he wrote to Fernando Toro in 1822: "I now belong to the Colombia family, and no longer to the Bolívar family; naturally I do not belong to Caracas, I belong to the whole nation."[22] In contrast, the behavior characteristic of the elites is clearly shown in the efforts made by the scholar Andrès Bello, who could imagine nothing more desirable than to have his own coffee plantation with slaves.[23]

From 1812 to the middle of 1813 and again from the middle of 1814 to 1821, Bolívar, as the leader of a "rebellion"—as it was called in the language of the Spanish Empire (connected with the juristic fact of high treason, on which the death sentence was based)—was denied access to his possessions and the revenues from the work done by his slaves.[24] First, the Spaniards sequestered the goods of their opponents, as did the patriots fighting for independence. Then they confiscated them and auctioned them off to the highest bidder, in order to finance the war. Those of Bolívar's slaves who had not escaped continued to work on the plantations and haciendas.

However, here too there is a familiar peculiarity that supporters of the Bolívar myth do not like to hear about, but which the Venezuelan historian Inés Quintero, for instance, never ceases to emphasize: Simón Bolívar's elder sister, María Antonia Bolívar Palacios y Blanco, opposed her brother's political ambitions, as did most of the Creole oligarchy. A faithful supporter of the Spanish king, she went into exile from 1814 to 1822 (primarily in Havana), and was rewarded by being given, among the Bolívar's family's possessions that the Spaniards had confiscated, two sugar plantations in Maca and a cocoa bean hacienda in the Tacarigua valleys, along with their male and female slaves, eleven buildings in La Guaira, and five in Caracas—all these providing a fairly large income.[25]

Strictly speaking, the war in Venezuela was fought from 1810 to 1821, with later flare-ups until 1824. But basically, once the violence had broken out, it continued during the rest of the nineteenth century. At first it looked as though war and violence would come to an end, since it was fought over the abolition of slavery. On June 24, 1821, the decisive battle for control of the central plantation region and the Caracas area took place near Carabobo. Bolívar's and Paéz's troops were victorious. However, on closer inspection of the documents, we see that none of the elite officers truly took the abolition of slavery seriously. In the exuberance of victory, Simón Bolívar freed six of his slaves at the San Mateo hacienda: María Jacinta Bolívar, José de la Luz Bolívar, María Bartola Bolívar, Francisca Bárbara Bolívar, Juan de la Rosa Bolívar, Nicolaza Bolívar.[26] But this was largely a symbolic gesture.

In a slaveholding society under the legal system of the Spanish Empire, *libertad* (the act of emancipation) had to be declared by means of an individual *carta de libertad* (letter of emancipation) for each slave, signed by the owner and emancipator before a notary and witnesses. In 1821, Bolívar did indeed carry out the act of emancipation on the San Mateo hacienda and orally declare his slaves to be free. But this emancipation was not recognized by the political and legal authorities controlled by other slaveholders. In any case, in 1827, when he was living in Caracas again, Bolívar had to either do the paperwork in accordance with the regulations (in Bolívar's private papers for 1821 there is no such document to be found[27]) or have the documentation ratified.[28] A formulation in the ratification of 1827 refers to the problems that the ex-slaves had between 1821 and 1827, in which the issue was the "own right" of the former slaves: "Juan de la Rosa and his wife, Nicolaza Bolívar, with the authorities and other undertakings in connection with their documentation, done in accord with their own right by Juan de la Rosa and María Jacinta Bolívar."[29]

These documents from 1827 regarding the six former slaves are the only ones signed by Bolívar as a slave-owner. All the other texts by him allude to slavery in general terms and only very covertly to his own slaves. They are speeches, writings, proclamations, and laws, such as the decree regarding "confiscation and liberation" of the slaves of the Ceiba Grande hacienda in Casanare, where Bolívar had temporarily established his headquarters in 1820.[30]

After 1821, most of the slaves that were part of Bolívar's personal property remained under his family's management as *manumismos* with slave status, if they had not escaped or disappeared. In Daniel F. O'Leary's notebook, we find an important comment regarding Bolívar's liberation of slaves, which shows on the one hand that he had already begun the actual emancipation (without notarized written documents) of male slaves on military grounds as early as 1814 (and not only in 1816). The comment also proves the previously mentioned liberation of slaves in 1827. However, the numbers are exaggerated: "During the 1814 military campaign the Liberator offered freedom to slaves who wanted to enter military service and also gave it to them. He began with his own, of whom about fifteen joined up. This decree was issued from April to June (1814). In 1821, after [the battle of] Carabobo, he gave it [freedom] unconditionally to all the San Mateo slaves, I don't recall the number, but it was not less than one hundred, and certainly it was even more than that. This time he did it orally, and when he returned from Peru [to Venezuela] in 1827, he provided those who were still alive with formal emancipation documents. He did this as a private individual in contrast to 1814, when he was a magistrate [basically, the head of the government—MZ] and could decide the matter, and he himself gave the example that was to be followed."[31]

On the whole, Bolívar left the management of his property to his nephew Anacleto Clemente Bolívar, the eccentric son of his eldest sister, María Antonia.[32] The Liberator did not concern himself with the complicated legal questions that arose from war, the policy of confiscation, and reconstruction. In 1824, when Bolívar was on his campaign in Peru, the task of managing the family's possessions was assigned to his eldest sister. María Antonia Palacios y Blanco's first official act was to have an *inventario de bienes* (property inventory) drawn up.[33] This inventory shows two things: first, that the old elite's latifundia economy was in poor condition after the long war; and second, that the drawing up of the inventory was the first step toward the economic reconstruction and restoration of the old elite's domination. By shifting his sphere of activity to the continental level, Simón Bolívar could keep his distance from this conservative process of reconstruction but not escape it. From 1821 to 1827, he remained outside Venezuela and also outside Great Colombia (which had itself been created in order to carry through necessary centralizing governmental reforms—a complete failure).

Venezuela's old elite, the urban oligarchy of the mantuanos, had been decimated during the war for independence. If we take the Bolívar family in Simón's generation as our example, we can say that in the war that lasted from 1810 to 1824 they had lost the true heir: the firstborn son, Juan Vicente Bolívar y Palacios. Also lost was Pablo Clemente Francia, the husband of, María Antonia Bolívar Palacios y Blanco, who was in exile in Cuba at the time of his death.

According to the 1824 inventory, the Bolívars owned the following haciendas, *hatos*, buildings, and mines: the Hacienda de San Mateo, the showpiece of the Bolívar *mayorazgo*; the *hato* El Totumo in the Llanos altos del Guárico; the Hacienda de Chirgua; several haciendas in the valley of the Tuy, including the Hacienda Palacios (Barlovento); the Hacienda de Santo Domingo; the Hacienda de Araguïta; the Hacienda de San Vicente and the haciendas

The Bolívar family house in San Mateo in the Aragua valley
(F. Bellermann, 1844).

of Macaita, Suata, and Caicara; buildings in La Guaira and one on the banks of the Guaire River; the family residence on the central square of Caracas;, and other buildings in the city.[34] In a notarized document, Simón Bolívar and his older sister made a binding agreement that Simón should have possession of the mines of Aroa (and Cocorote) as well as two buildings in Caracas. María Antonia Bolívar was to have the haciendas "de caña y café" in San Mateo as well as the haciendas of Suata and Caicara, with the specification "que ninguna de ellas tiene esclavitud" (that none of them will have slavery).[35] Whether this provision was observed, we do not know.

One detail may make it clearer how the old elites restored their domination using the same techniques they had used before 1810. In 1821, Anacleto Clemente, who benefited most from the Bolívar family heritage, married Rosa Rodriguez del Toro y Toro, the niece of his brother Rodríguez del Toro (the Marqués del Toro, etc.), whose mother was in addition a relative of Bolívar's wife who had died young.[36] This connection was nothing other than an attempt to keep the upper level of society exclusive by means of endogamous marriage strategies. Through its microscopic vision, history writ small can serve as a corrective to macrohistory. Another detail: in a letter of October 9, 1821, written from Rosario de Cúcuta, Bolívar requests that his nephew Anacleto Clemente give his "former servant Dionisio" (servant = slave), if he wants to *"trabajar la tierra"* (work the land) as much *"que necesite en mi poseción de Suata, para que la cultive sin pagar, por ahora, en arrendamiento, hasta que yo lo disponga"* (as he needs on my estate of Suata, so that he can cultivate it [the land], without paying for it, for now, in leasehold, until I make a decision about it).[37] This was, as in the colonies of the last phase of the Roman Empire, the presupposition for the transition from direct slavery to forms of peonage in which serfs were bound to the land in a kind of debt-slavery. The Suata hacienda, which belonged to Bolívar, lay in the south of the main estate of San Mateo. In 1810, Bolívar had begun to grow *añil* (indigo) for export, which required a large labor force. After the destruction resulting from the battles between 1810 and 1821, the owners needed to bring in independent workers to rebuild their haciendas. Regarding Dionisio, we find in the *Escritos del Libertador* the following comment: "Sergeant Dionisio Bolívar, ex-slave of the family whose name he bore in accord with the customs of the time, was at this time the Liberator's majordomo and was in Rosario de Cúcuta."[38]

In the famous 1830 will, the financial circumstances of 1824 and 1827 are once again established; Bolívar names the rest of his family as "únicos universales herederos" (sole universal heirs).[39] More precisely, this refers to his "Sisters María Antonia and Juana Bolívar and the children of my brother Juan Vicente Bolívar, namely Juan, Felicia and Fernando Bolívar."[40] In 1830, Bolívar still owned only the copper mines in Aroa.

These copper mines were the greatest problem connected with the family fortune. They were—because they were not profitable—abandoned by the Bolívars even before 1800. The mines hardly produced anything anymore, but they were still nominally part of the family property (Humboldt had made notes on this). And in colonial Spanish America, land law certainly had a clause regarding the "responsibility for and productivity of property."[41] In 1804, a woman from the Basque country, Francisca Zagarzasu, had owned the valley of Aroa and the mines. After 1821, the Bolívar family was involved in complicated legal actions regarding this part of the inheritance.

An essential aspect of the Bolívar myth concerns the attitude of the slaveholder Bolívar toward slavery and toward his own slaves. Between 1814 and 1816, and even in 1821, Bolívar had certainly issued proclamations, decrees, and other legal actions that struck at the root of slavery, even though he was a member of an extremely conservative latifundia elite. He did so for military reasons and in order to ensure the survival of the independence movement, but it remains undeniable that he did it.[42] On closer inspection, however, we see that these acts remained discursively on the level of the state and had little or no effect on social reality. The available notarial records of the emancipations suggest that Bolívar symbolically freed six people. This act already aroused resistance and cost him considerable effort, as we have already seen. He could not prevent certain developments that shaped the socioeconomic structure and actually attempted to do so only in two or three letters or brief addresses.

Since about 1780, slavery in Venezuela had been in crisis. After 1821, this led elite families like the Bolívars to try to keep their haciendas and *mayorazgos* undivided, in order to safeguard their status. Because of their victory in the revolution for independence, they succeeded in doing so, at least until the crisis of the 1840s—in spite of the formal cancellation of the Spanish *mayorazgos* law ("cesen los vinculos y mayorazgos en Colombia"[43]), the unprofitability of the great landed estates, and other difficulties.[44] The large estate also produced considerable profits when demand on the other side of the Atlantic was high (as it was between 1821 and 1842 and again in the 1870s). Only after 1842 did foreigners, tenants, and businessmen increasingly take over the traditional haciendas. That the latter were at the same time status symbols is shown not least by the fact that the most powerful representatives of the old elites and then also politicians and caudillos owned the largest haciendas, such as the great Hacienda Trinidad near Caracas, which before 1810 had belonged to the Marqués de Casa León, later to José Antonio Páez, then to President Cipriano Castro, and finally to the dictator Juan Vicente Gómez.[45]

On the other hand, the "crisis of slavery" does not mean that the dominant families really gave up their property rights to their slaves—despite the quasi-revolutionary discourses of the revolution for independence.[46] What did that mean for Simón Bolívar and his family's ownership of slaves? It's very simple: he freed the slaves (the precise number is unknown) of the Mayorazgo San Mateo and the Mayorazgo de la Concepción: "dación de la libertad a sus esclavos" (granting of freedom to his slaves), to use the legal formula.[47] But since between 1824 and 1827 Bolívar handed over all his lands to his family, the slaves on the other estates—insofar as Bolívar had not taken them to war with him—remained in slavery or were, according to the official language of the Congress of Cúcuta (1821), "freed slaves." As we have seen, this basically changed only the name by which slaves were called, not their reality. For that reason, the clause in the 1827 contract between Simón Bolívar and his sister María Antonia that specifies "that none of them [the estates] practices slavery"[48] is also less clear than it at first appears to be. Were the people who were subject to "servitude" simply no longer there, having escaped or gone to war? Or were they no longer called *esclavos* (slaves) in 1827, but rather *manumismos*, who were still subject to a veiled form of slavery?

The emancipation of his slaves and his personal aversion to slavery represent above all the foundations for the Bolívar myth in the oral version of the Venezuelan underclass memory. Made heroic in the stories about "El Negro Primero" or Manuelote, who were in reality bodyguards and symbolized the few black slaves in the Llanos of Venezuela, this version was disseminated chiefly by José Antonio Páez's memoirs. At the same time, Bolívar's ritual gestures of freedom involved a severe criticism of his class and particularly of his family—very specifically, of his overbearing sister María Antonia, who said herself that she "held the family fortune together."[49]

In the individual case, the emancipation of Simón Bolívar's slaves meant two things: the young men who joined in the continental campaign died or else, with a little luck, might have risen to become tenants after the war, like the previously mentioned Dionisio. For Bolívar's other slaves (older men, women, and children) emancipation did not mean that they could control their own lives. On the contrary, though they were now called *manumismos,* most of them remained slaves on the haciendas or became peons. All of them were formally *ciudadanos* (citizens) but continued to be subject to their respective masters.

Bolívar included a further authority in his radical centralism, primarily in order to prevent regional large-estate owners, to whom slaves and peons might also belong, from having too much influence.

His attitude is best seen in a letter to Francisco Santander written from San Carlos on June 13, 1821, just a week before the battle of Carabobo:

> Here people know little about the Congress of Cúcuta [where manumission was decided upon]: it is said that many want to join the Cundinamarca federation; but I am consoled by the fact that neither you [Santander] nor Nariño, nor Zea, nor I, nor Paéz, nor many other venerable authorities that the liberation army has, are favorable to such a delirium.... The scribblers [i.e., intellectuals—MZ] think that the will of the people is their opinion, without knowing that in Colombia the people is in the army, because it really is there and because [the army] has wrested this people from the hands of the tyrants; because furthermore it is the people that wants something, the people that works, and the people that can do something; the rest are people who go on vegetating with more or less malice or more or less patriotism, but all of them without any right to be other than passive citizens. This politics, which is certainly not that of Rousseau, will ultimately have to be developed so that those gentlemen [the scribblers]

> don't ruin everything again ... the second part [sought by the scribblers—MZ] is that of the Guárico.[50] These gentlemen think that Colombia is full of sheep comfortably bundled up in the stove-heated rooms of Bogotá, Tunja, and Pamplona. They have not considered the Caribs from the Orinoco, the shepherds of Apure [Llaneros], the [colored] mariners of Maracaibo, the boatmen of the Magdalena River, the bandits of Patia, the untamed Pastusos, the Guajibo Indians of Casanare, and all the savage hordes from Africa and America that, like deer, roam the wastelands of Colombia.[51]

Bolívar made it quite clear that in the Bolívarian centralized state, all *manumismos*, all cities, and also all quasi-autonomous societies in resistance and the quasi-autonomous clientele of local large-estate owners would be brought under the control of the army. In the political system, these people were to be allowed to play only the role of passive citizens.

As in every slaveholding society, the emancipated young male slaves who were now soldiers continued to be part of the clientele of their former owners, as had basically been the common practice since the time of Roman slavery. This also held for the slaves that belonged to Simón Bolívar and his family and whom Bolívar had taken with him on his continental campaign. Here, even the stereotype of "ultimate slaves" (Orlando Patterson) was accurate—for the bodyguards. Since 1819, a certain José Bolívar had been a member of Simón Bolívar's entourage. He was a descendent of former slaves belonging to the Bolívar clan and who lived on one of the Bolívars' *hatos*. In battle, José Bolívar rose to become an officer. During the whole of the Peruvian campaign, this black captain was one of Simón Bolívar's bodyguards. He often served as the Liberator's emissary and personal messenger, which shows how much Simón Bolívar trusted him.

In 1827, when the conflicts between Bolívarianos and Santanderistas were growing more intense, José Bolívar publicly beat up, on a street in Bogotá, his boss's main journalistic enemy, the "scribbler" Vicente Aguero, the director of the paper *El Conductor*.

In March 1828, the unintended perfidy of post-abolitionist independence reached its high point: José Bolívar was sent to Cartagena to bring the arrested Admiral José Padilla, a war hero and a dark-skinned pardo with decidedly republican ideas, to Bogotá for judgment. Shortly thereafter, Padilla was shot—by a republican firing squad. Then José Bolívar once again performed the role of the loyal messenger—he informed Simón Bolívar that he had been named dictator. This descendent of the Bolívar family's slaves crowned his career as a bodyguard on September 25, 1828, when he shielded his master with his own body and was killed.[52] One can deny neither of them fame; the underlying models of conduct, circumstances, structures, and mentalities were those of a slaveholding society,

Throughout his life, Simón Bolívar behaved in accord with the rules of this society. His speeches and habitus also conformed to its norms—precisely because this society was undergoing rapid political change. Only in his speeches and views regarding the latifundium and slavery, and not in his treatment of *manumismos* and former slaves, did he distance himself from his group, the slaveholding elite of the great estates.

The Conservative-Romantic Bolívar Myth

Simón Bolívar loved great entrances, rituals, speeches, gestures, dances, and receptions. When the patriotic troops had liberated a city, the general liked to have his carriage of honor drawn by virgins who celebrated him with festivities and triumphal arches. During his own lifetime, Bolívar himself initiated a patriotic cult. The year 1813 marked the beginning; the first elements of the Bolívar myth were also part of this early cult.

Anastasio Girardot (1791–1813), one of the Creole officers from New Granada who had supported Bolívar since his march on Caracas in 1813 (Campaña Admirable), had died in heavy fighting near Valencia. On the evening of the same day, Bolívar had already written a communiqué stating that Girardot's heart was to be "conveyed in the triumphal procession into the capital Caracas, …

where it was to be received by the Liberator and deposited in a mausoleum [to be] erected in the Caracas cathedral."[53]

On October 14, 1813, the urn bearing the heart was carried through Caracas to the cathedral. Simón Bolívar, brigadier general of the Venezuelan army; Narciso Coll y Prat (1754–1822), the Catalan second archbishop of Caracas,[54] rather unwillingly; and Cristóbal Mendoza (1722–1829), the political governor of the state of Venezuela, presided over the ceremony. In the course of the festivities, Mendoza spoke, emphasizing Bolívar's achievements and recommending that the Asamblea (assembly of citizens), "in the name of the people," promote Bolívar to a higher military rank than that of brigadier general. He also suggested that Bolívar should be given "an epithet or byname that will perpetuate his memory in the annals of free America."[55] The Asamblea thereupon decided to appoint Bolívar "Captain General of the Army of Venezuela ... with all the rights and privileges of this military rank," and at the same time to give him the "byname of Liberator of Venezuela." The portals of all *municipalidades* (mayoral offices) were to be adorned with the inscription "Bolívar Libertador de Venezuela."

In the early cult, the power to command, military status, and the honor of a captain general went hand in hand with the patriotic honorary title of Libertador—and all this in an invented "Roman" tradition. Thenceforth Bolívar bore the title of Libertador. In 1813, he himself created the Orden de los Liberadores, into which primarily successful generals and military men were inducted.

Between 1821 and 1830, Bolívar as Libertador was once again the object of a kind of early Bolívar cult, by which the elites, especially in the cities through which the Liberator passed on his campaigns, sought to manipulate him by means of praise and luxury. The legacies of this patriotic cult of the victor were, above all, a large number of portraits and medals (1819–1829) that gave the Bolívar myth a visual foundation.[56] Most of the portraits, both those produced in Bogotá and those produced in Caracas (1827), were painted by nonacademic craftsman-painters who were pardos. These included Pedro José Figueroa (1770–1838) and José María Espinosa (1796–1883) in Bogotá and Juan Lovera (1776–1841) in

Caracas.⁵⁷ For the most part, the pardo craftsmen adhered to the tradition of colonial religious painting and wood carving (chiefly of Catholic saints[58]). After the patriots' victory, pictures of them, clearly painted in the style of depictions of the saints, were in great demand. Juan Lovera had learned his craft from the Dominicans in the convent of San Jacinto and from the painter–master craftsman Antonio José Landaeta. After 1821, Lovera, an eyewitness to the "liberation" of Caracas, gave up painting saints and Christian symbols and turned toward the patriot heroes. He painted some of the most important "founding fathers" of Venezuela: Cristóbal Mendoza, Mariano Herrera Toro, and Casimiro Vegas. When he returned temporarily to Caracas in 1827, Lovera probably painted a portrait of Bolívar as well.[59]

We also owe to Juan Lovera the two famous pictures *El 19 de abril de 1810* (depicting the founding of the Caracas junta), painted in 1835, and *El 5 de julio de 1811* (depicting the declaration of independence), painted in 1837.[60] They pay homage to the beginnings of Independencia in its mythical version, but still without Bolívar. In the 1830s, the elites did not think much of the recently deceased Libertador. On the other hand, during Bolívar's lifetime, they had still sought to marry their daughters to Bolivarian colonels or generals—the city of Quito had been particularly successful in this respect.

Finally, regarding these early developments of the Bolívar cult, which provided the first elements for the visual myth of Bolívar, we must mention that in a hitherto largely overlooked letter written to the Prussian diplomat Christian Carl Josias Bunsen in 1830, Alexander von Humboldt clearly referred to the effects this cult had had on the governmental experiments. Commenting on Bolívar's resignation and retirement, Humboldt noted that the Libertador had withdrawn "from an arena in which his presence weakened all belief in institutions, because people always looked only to him and expected everything from him."[61]

The cult of Bolívar in the whole of Colombia during his lifetime came quickly to an end. As Libertador-president (1828–1830), Simón Bolívar tried to hold the state of Great Colombia against the interests of the "normal" oligarchies. From 1828 to 1830, Bolívar was treated, above all by the founders of the new "old" Venezuela (appeal was explicitly made to the "old" colonial boundaries), as a "dead dog." Until 1840, Bolívar was considered Public Enemy No. 1. But he returned to life, thanks to the popular imagination. From 1842 on, when new oligarchic Venezuela was in the grip of the Atlantic economic crisis, the dead Libertador had to serve as the charismatic social revolutionary that the real Bolívar had never been. Against the bitter opposition of the anti-Bolívarians, President Paéz, who as a Llanero leader had himself once been an emancipator of slaves, had the dead Libertador brought home as a new "god."

Bolívar's bones were brought back to Caracas and interred in its cathedral, where he had been baptized, while the urn with the remains of his heart remained in Santa Marta. Venezuela's republican-patriotic ancestor cult, founded by Páez and his advisers, then got into high gear. Making use of his knowledge of the orally transmitted history of the Llanos in the civil war, Páez integrated into the conservative myth a series of social-revolutionary and romantic elements. He also tried, unsuccessfully, to have Caracas renamed Ciudad Bolívar. The conservative elites' willingness to compromise did not extend that far. In the end, however, the cult's first two memorial sites were established: the baptistery where Bolívar's bones were interred, which is now the National Pantheon and is located near the National Library, and the Plaza Bolívar in Angostura/Ciudad Bolívar, which is today the center of that Venezuelan city.

The Plaza Bolívar is probably the Bolívar cult's most important memorial site. Its origin lies in the local Bolívar myth of the wonderful Orinoco town of Angostura. In the nineteenth century, that town was long dominated by liberal elites that invoked Bolívar's work there, the constitutional tradition, and the Congress of Angostura (1819). Whereas the beautiful original name of the town has been reserved chiefly for bitters made there, the Plaza Bolívar in Ciudad Bolívar has become the model for all the Plazas Bolívar in Venezuela (and elsewhere). The heart of this memorial site is a statue of Bolívar, in most cities an equestrian monument, and in smaller localities often a standing statue or bust.

In the ritual of bringing home the dead hero, we can already see many elements of the Bolívar cult as a kind of civil state religion. Twelve years after his death, Bolívar was given the burial honors of a captain general. After a sea voyage in November and December 1842, the mortal remains finally reached Bolívar's native city, where they were received by large crowds. They were interred in the chapel of the Santísima Trinidad church, everything was hung with black crepe, with Venezuelan flags here and there and Phrygian caps on the flagpoles as symbols of freedom.

On the anniversary of Bolívar's death, December 17, President Páez, the "Lion of the Llanos," his ministers, troops, representatives of the Church, and foreign consuls and diplomats assembled in front of the chapel. Bolívar's bones were carried to the Church of San Francisco in a ceremonial procession. Finally Bolívar's remains were taken to the cathedral on December 23, 1842, and laid to rest there in the family crypt.

Páez also failed in his attempt to get the anniversary of Bolívar's death declared a national holiday. His chief opponent in this effort was Dr. Ángel Quintero, a minister and one of Páez's main advisers who had recommended Bolívar's proscription in 1830. Thus not until 1874 could the Santísima Trinidad Church be declared by President Guzmán Blanco as the Panteón Nacional.

A decree issued by President Páez also ordered Bolívar's return to the Palace of Government and the Congress—at least in the form of a statue of European marble. The committee that organized this Bolívar ritual consisted of General Francisco Rodríguez del Toro (1761–1851), General Mariano Montilla (1782–1851), and the former president José María Vargas (1786–1854). The paraphernalia used in the transfer (hearse, triumphal arches, etc.)—and here we see the elites' orientation toward European high culture—were ordered in Paris by the military geographer and surveyor Agustín Codazzi (1793–1854). Daniel Florencio O'Leary commissioned Pietro Tenerani in Rome to make the marble monument to Bolívar.[62] Liberals and conservatives unanimously agreed that the local craftsmen and stonecutters, who were all pardos, would be incapable of carrying out such important works. Not least, these works were intended to overwrite, as it were, the pictures made by pardo craftsmen in the 1820s and to replace them with a new visual memory of new memorial sites.

The most important elements of the governmental elite's new, ceremonial Bolívar cult were already available, but they were not completely assembled until the beginning of the 1870s. Only at that time were the presuppositions for a new function of the Bolívar myth met. It is not clear whether versions of the Bolívar myth that are now widespread in many variant forms had already emerged from the oral tradition. But that seems likely when they are compared with the tradition of icons and figures of the saints, which were created by pardos working in the oral tradition of Venezuela's legends.

A marvelous example of the folk myth about Simón Bolívar is the story of his birth as the son of a black female slave living in Capaya (Tuy valley), one of the Caracas elite's most important cocoa-bean-growing regions. The Bolívar family owned the Hacienda Palacios there. According to this story, Simón is supposed to have been given as an infant to his (actual) mother, Concepción, who was at the hacienda during the last weeks of her pregnancy and whose own child had died shortly after birth.[63] In Venezuela, slavery was formally abolished only in 1854. The myth conforms to the discourse of resistance and is part of a republicanism from below, directed against the veiled reconstruction of slavery that took place between 1821 and 1832, following Bolívar's abolition decrees (starting in 1816).

Further official sites memorializing Bolívar gradually emerged. It is noteworthy that many modernizations, such as electric lights, were first introduced in the Bolívar monuments or at least tried out in his name. Venezuela, and in part Colombia, was covered with Bolívar statues that also became a major export item for Venezuela.

The collections of Bolívar's documents, letters, speeches, decrees, and writings, combined with *memorias* (memories) of his most important comrades in arms, were designated as "Archivos" or "Escritos" and mostly issued in multiple volumes with large printings. These also acquired substantial significance for the conservative myth. In the 1860s, José Antonio Páez and his advisers had already tried, using Páez's own *Memorias*, to legitimate the conservative oligarchies' rule retroactively, so to speak. After the liberals gained dominance in Venezuela (starting about 1864), each president (almost) made himself eternal with a Bolívar archive. These archives in book form were (and are) a kind of portable Bolívar myth. In the 1870s, the conception of the state changed and, along with it, the function of the myth and cult. President Antonio Guzmán Blanco (his administration, from 1870 to 1888, is also called Guzmanato) distinguished himself in this respect by having himself called an *autocrata civilizador* (civilizing autocrat). He modernized election law (since 1875, there had been universal suffrage for all men twenty-one and over, but with a multileveled process for electing the president) and strengthened civil marriage. He created new law books, introduced universal compulsory education, and instituted the first real national census (1873 and 1881). He invested in newspapers, the construction of roads and railroads, telegraphs, and other blessings of modernity—which began in the West around 1870.

One of the greatest achievements of the Guzmanato consisted in the standardization of the monetary system—which also provides a tangible symbol of the now massively practiced Bolívar cult (in 1880, the fiftieth anniversary of Bolívar's death was celebrated; in 1883, the centennial of his birth).[64] From the country's three or four local ersatz currencies circulating around the peso and the macuquina, Guzmán Blanco created a new Bolívar coin, the bolívar de plata (silver bolívar, 1879). The coin was initially known as the peso venezolano, and in 1882 its value was set at five French silver francs.[65] The fact that the close connection with Bolívar's name and myth could become a problem was shown by the massive devaluation of the Bolívar after 1983, coinciding, embarrassingly enough, with the two hundredth anniversary of the Libertador's birth.

In any case, it is clear that the Bolívar myth first officially entered the elitist historical canon in the last third of the nineteenth century. The already existing elements of the myth and of the "people's Bolívar" did not absolutely contradict the official image of Bolívar. Often they were related symbiotically to one another. The popular myth assimilated and reinterpreted in everyday language the concepts of the conservative and social revolutionary myth, which again had taken over elements of the popular myth. Whatever did not find its way into any of the myths, or if it did, then only as a submyth of "rich man who fights the poor," were Bolívar's oligarchic ancestry and his continuing interest in the bases of this elitist status. For nineteenth-century conservatives who felt themselves to be associated, in terms of intellectual history, with the Enlightenment, Bolívar had to at least belong to the liberal constitutional tradition (the break with the Enlightenment did not come until the twentieth century, in the work of Vallenilla Lanz). And the popular myth denied Bolívar's oligarchic roots, because in the myth he was alleged to be the son or grandson of a black female slave and "did not accept the way the Spaniards treated slaves."[66]

Modernity began around 1870 in literature and historiography as well. The physician, naturalist, costumbrist, and historian Arístides Rojas (1826–1894) published, under the banner of the positivism imported to Venezuela by Germans, works in which he meticulously collected mores and customs, and recorded idioms and orally transmitted memories. In 1842, the sixteen-year-old Rojas had witnessed the return of Bolívar's mortal remains. He was then a student at the most famous elite institution, the Colegio de la Independencia, founded by the former royalist Feliciano Montenegro y Colón. One of his classmates was the young Antonio Guzmán Blanco. Roja's first work bore the title *Ciencia y poesía* (1868). In it Rojas could hardly escape the powerful pull of Venezuela's popular culture, to which poetry presumably belongs as well. Out of the collected oral materials, he constructed "conversations" like the one that is supposed to have taken place between Humboldt and Bolívar in Paris in 1804.

Rojas's writings about Humboldt were published in the newspaper *La Opinion Nacional* in 1879 and 1880, when the yellow liberals were also definitively establishing themselves in Venezuela. Rojas's discoveries were put into circulation as well by the widely distributed *Almanaque para todos* (1875–1882), a literature almanac. The first article about Humboldt bore the title "La casa de Humboldt en Caracas" (The Humboldt house in Caracas).

Rojas also polished up literarily another encounter through whose representation a strong current of legitimation was to flow over the new nation: the meeting of Andrés Bello and the "barón Alejandro de Humboldt": "Bello, then a young man of eighteen, was introduced to the traveler and won his heart with the first conversation in French that he began with him. When the Prussian saw how this heart was moved by the sense of the beautiful and love for nature, he held out his hand to him [Bello] and encouraged him with flattering remarks."[67] Apart from the fact that Humboldt was neither a "baron" nor, what now is closer, a "*Freiherr*,"[68] it would have to be shown that Bello spoke French and that (European) high culture was not poorly cultivated in Caracas. For his concept of the nation Rojas thought he needed to convey such encounters literally, encounters that had actually occurred but whose content no one really knew. Such encounters were either only memories in the heads of those who were present or *rumores* (rumors, gossip).

Rojas's idealizations were once again incorporated into the Bolívar myth and acquired the status of sources for historical research.[69] Today it is recognized that Rojas had a "sentido fundacional de la nacionalidad"[70] (a fundamental sense for nationality) and was a pioneer in Venezuelan historiography. Orality and the Bolívar myth are part of this sense of nationality. When the Cuban poet José Martí (1853–1895) spent a few months in Caracas in 1881, he borrowed a great deal from Arístides Rojas, including his method of incorporating myths, oral memories, and legends into the written culture and transforming them.[71]

In 1881, Eduardo Blanco's epic *Venezuela heroica* also appeared. This was a collection of stories about the war for independence in which oral memories were put down in writing. Much of what appears therein had been told to the author by General Antonio Páez himself.[72]

The various oral or previously unpublished *memorias* concealed a significant legitimating potential and, even today, represent an immense reservoir of myths. Thus Antonio Guzmán Blanco authorized the publication of the most important Bolívar documents: the documents collected by Bolívar's adjutant Daniel Florencio O'Leary along with his memories in the form of a narrative (though he did not authorize publication of the third volume, which contains the years between 1826 and 1830, the "betrayal of Bolívar" by the Venezuelan elites and by Páez).[73] The *Documentos para la historia de la vida pública del Libertador*, by José Félix Blanco and Ramón Azpurúa, were also published between 1875 and 1877.[74] Venezuela's "second religion," the Bolívar myth, was given a firm foundation proceeding from archives and texts that were in communication with the oral memory. Guzmán Blanco also selected the patriotic song "Gloria al Bravo Pueblo" as Venezuela's national anthem. Under President Juan Vicente Gómez, the archives published under Guzmán Blanco's government were supplemented by *Cartas de Bolívar*,[75] selected by Vicente Lecuna (1870–1954), and other Bolívar documents published under Gómez's successors as well.[76] Vicente Lecuna, the high priest of the myth and of the pictorial art cult in the first half of the twentieth century, had, like Vallenilla Lanz and a few other positivistic intellectuals, publicly opted for the Gómez dictatorship. In this period, Venezuela became one of Latin America's leading economic powers, and because of the oil boom, it had the money necessary for a new myth of stabilization. Stabilization also caused poverty, because the country was actually undergoing development for the first time as a result of the rise in the number of immigrants it attracted.

The various forms of the Bolívar cult and the myths regarding Bolívar and other leading figures of Independencia were never merely a past historical memory but instead a living and important part of politics and culture in Venezuela. Before the beginning of Chavist Bolívarism and the foundation of the Bolívarian republic, the idea of archiving Bolívar documents reached its temporary peak with the publication of all the texts going back to Bolívar—the *Escritos del Libertador*,[77] a century-long project begun in 1938 by the Sociedad Bolívariana de Venezuela. Standing in the tradition of the great Bolívar projects from Monagas to Gómez, the *Escritos* are the most important document of the Bolívar myth that appeared between 1950 and 1990. Its editor, Cristobal L. Mendoza, not only held the leading position in the Academia Nacional de la Historia from 1933 to 1973 but also served as president of the Sociedad Bolívariana de Venezuela and chair of the editorial committee of the *Escritos del Libertador* (1949–1964 and 1964–1974, respectively). He embodied the continuing existence of a version of the Bolívar myth that had in the meantime become extremely conservative, and also the continuity of the old oligarchic elite of Caracas. In 1811, his great-grandfather Cristóbal Mendoza had been president of the First Republic and, in 1813, created the title of Libertador for Bolívar.[78]

In addition to the Simón Bolívar plazas that represented the urban architectural and spatial dimension of the myth, and the archives that more scientifically supported the myth for positivist intellectuals, other memorial sites were also created for the cult. Besides the Pantheon in Caracas and the Plaza Bolívar found in every locality, Guzmán Blanco had Bolívar's *casa natal* (the house where he was born) restored.[79] The university graduate Antonio Guzmán Blanco, who spoke with French novelists in their own language but who could also swear like a caudillo, became, after José Antonio Páez, the second founder of the cult of the apotheosized Libertador. However, even this more liberal version remained within the framework of the mythical conservative-romantic Bolívar. Guzmán Blanco turned the Bolívar myth into a museum object and promoted the visualization of the Bolívar cult.

Martín Tovar y Tovar (1827–1902), who came from an aristocratic family and had been educated in Madrid and Paris, opened, in collaboration with José Antonio Salas, the Studio Fotografía Artística—where Tovar painted portraits from photographs—and combined the art of painting with the then highly modern art of photography.[80] He had made his mark as a painter of historical pictures (e.g., *Escena llanera*).[81] Guzmán Blanco commissioned him to decorate the Palacio Federal (Palace of Government) in Caracas with scenes from the history of Venezuela. In this way, the imagination of the great heroes and important events in national history received their own format and their own formal language. For example, Tovar created the historical pictures *La firma del Acta de la Independencia* (The Signing of the Declaration of Independence) and *La Batalla de Carabobo* (The Battle of Carabobo).[82] In the large format visualization, ritual swank was combined with foreign design and material, particularly in 1883, on the occasion of the centenary of Bolívar's birth. It was part of an extensive program of urban modernization, especially in Caracas (the Capitolio and the Palacio Federal, with paintings by Martín Tovar y Tovar)—the result is the historic center of modern-day Caracas. But a "Caracas-ization" of architecture, infrastructure, and politics took place in the rest of the country as well.[83] The painter Arturo Michelena (1863–1898), who went to Paris in 1885 and remained there for four years, devoted himself more generally to historical painting, but with his *Miranda en la Carraca* he shaped a subdivision of the Bolívar myth, that of the "fallen Miranda."[84]

Under Juan Vicente Gómez, the myth arrived in 1913 at a further stage of museification and visualization. In order to legitimate his dictatorship, the new president activated a cult of Bolívar as a soldier. Gómez defeated the caudillos who had entangled Venezuela in civil wars, rebellions, and crises throughout the nineteenth century. With a professionalized army, he actually refounded the Venezuelan state on the basis of a conservative Páez-and-Bolívar myth. This army was the sole truly national institution that Venezuela had at the beginning of the twentieth century; it was in a sense the skeleton of the state. Grounds for legitimation were provided not least by the centenaries of Independencia (1910 and 1930).[85] In 1930, on the occasion of the centenary of Bolívar's death, Gómez presented the repayment of the country's debts as the culmination of the Bolivarian quest for freedom.[86] He literally took himself to be Bolívar.

Under Gómezism, between 1913 and 1931, Bolívar's birthplace, and later also the National Pantheon, was decorated at great expense with splendid historical works by the painter Tito Salas

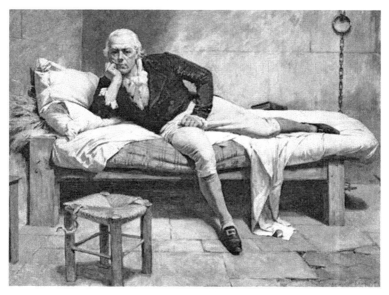

Miranda's Last Days in the Prison at La Carraca, Cádiz, based on a painting by Arturo Michelena, *La Carraca (1896).*

(1887–1974), whose real name was Británico Antonio Salas Díaz, the son of a brewer. Basically, the point was to present texts in paintings. Vicente Lecuna provided the themes. Salas and Lecuna pursued, naturally "in the manner of Europe's best painters" (Lecuna), a gigantic iconization of the Bolívar cult, creating the painting *Humboldt and Bolívar in Paris (1804),* for example. At the same time, the cult pictures also had didactic functions.[87] The subsidiary myths were further developed as well, as in the case of the—very much more modest—cult of Francisco de Miranda, the "most cosmopolitan of all Venezuelans."[88] Here, too, a canon was constructed, chiefly on the basis of the previously mentioned picture by Arturo Michelena. The museification and visualization of the Bolívar myth went so far that the collective memory of Simón Bolívar and the independence movement has always referred to these images, created between fifty and one hundred years after Bolívar's death. The establishment of sites, texts, and images of the conservative Bolívar myth and cult was almost complete in the

1970s, at the height of the so-called Punto Fijo democracy. Under its first president, Rafael Caldera (1916–2009), the golden age of state redistribution of wealth began, accompanied by a massive expansion of the Bolívar myth. On February 15, 1971, the anniversary of Bolívar's speech in Angostura, President Caldera issued a decree establishing the following: "Article 1: From 1971 on, in the week in which February 15 falls, Bolívar Studies Week will be observed in all the Republic's education institutions. Article 2: Bolívar Studies Week is to serve to analyze objectively the Libertador's actions and ideas and to remember him personally with the appropriate praise."[89] The program of Bolívar Studies Week was supposed to be adapted to the type and level of the educational institution concerned. To this end, a relatively thin book with the most important Bolívar documents was printed and distributed in large numbers, the costs being covered by oil revenues, of course. It was expressly declared that these documents were "speeches, reports, announcements, resolutions, declarations, decrees, regulations, statements, sayings, records, newspaper articles,"[90] forming a portable Bolívar archive, so to speak, but "without the scholarly apparatus of footnotes, indications of sources, and bibliographical references."[91] Since the two most important Bolívar scholars, Dr. Pedro Gual and Professor Manuel Pérez Vila, signed off on the selection, the "authenticity and reliability of the materials"[92] was assured. The book represented the "essence of his teaching."[93] Bolívar was expected once again to pacify the country after the guerilla battles of the 1960s and the student protests of 1968. And in a certain sense, this succeeded. In about 1972, political peace returned, and even the Leninist left seemed to have been provisionally integrated.

Between 1980 and 1983 (the 150th anniversary of Bolívar's death and the 200th anniversary of his birth), large conferences were held, and still another comprehensive archive was put together and subsequently published under the title *Bolívar and Europe*.[94] Various smaller projects followed, such as an institute with its own journal (the Bolívarium), diverse dictionaries and anthologies concerning Bolívar[95] and the *Decretos de Bolívar*.[96]

In its extremely conservative form, the myth legitimated a positivistic scientific and governmental culture whose various versions constituted for the general populace a kind of bible from which the apotheosized Liberator's words, messages, sayings and maxims could be obtained and parroted, especially in elementary schools.

In addition, however, a noncanonical oral version of the myth about Bolívar continued to exist that was connected with questions about slavery and veiled racism as well as with fighters like the peasant general Ezequiel Zamora; Llaneros opposing the Gómez dictatorship, such as "Maisanta," Hugo Chávez's grandfather;[97] and the guerillas of the 1960s.

However, many leftist intellectuals took no interest in Bolívar, and this went along with their condemnation of bloodless positivism. After the end of the Gómez dictatorship and under the new dictatorship of Marcos Pérez Jiménez (1952–1958), antimilitarism was also expressed as anti-Bolívarism. This attitude was largely adopted by the historians of the "social history generation." For them, the Bolívar cult was either ossified academicism, disguised militarism, or a kind of civil religion functioning as "the opium of the people."

From the "Marxist" to the "Democratic" Bolívar and Back

A Marxist interpretation of the Bolívar myth had a hard time challenging the state's conservative use of the myth. In the wave of revolutionary democratizations in the 1920s (likewise a phase of rebellion against the old liberal elites) that took hold in opposition to right-wing liberal dictatorships allied with the United States in Cuba (Gerardo Machado) but still more in Venezuela (Gómez), national history and its heroes were reevaluated. In Cuba, it was Julio A. Mella (1903–1929) who reclaimed not only José Marti but also Bolívar for an avant-gardist Latin American left.[98]

The most important Venezuelan activists and intellectuals involved in this reevaluation carried out by the radical left were Carlos Irazábal (1907–1991) and Rómulo Betancourt (1908–1981).[99]

Salvador de la Plaza, Gustavo Machado, Miguel Acosta Saignes, and Manuel Matos Romero also helped lay the foundations for a new conception of history. Carlos Irazábal set the strategic course with his *Hacia la democracia* (1939),[100] a very crude application of the Marxist theory of economic social formations to the history of Venezuela. In contrast, Betancourt, who favored caudillos and Stalinists, made history with a pistol in his hand and appealed to the activist Bolívar of the leftists. He also sought to drive out Vallenilla Lanz's ghost. With the motto "We do not respect the dead when they don't deserve any respect," Betancourt in 1936 accused the recently deceased Vallenilla Lanz of intellectual prostitution.[101]

To underpin the battle against the dictator Juan Vicente Gómez and his successors, three great theoretical complexes of the Bolívar myth had to be delegitimated or reinterpreted: the extreme conservative-militarist Bolívar of the Gomecistas, his positivist-clientelist form in the *Cesarismo democrático* (1919) written by Laureano Vallenilla Lanz, and Marx's short article "Bolivar y Ponte," which had been published in 1936 in Buenos Aires by Anibal Ponce.[102] This triple deconstruction of the Bolívar myth was a protracted process, from which today's "Chavist Bolívar" emerged, in a sense. Nonetheless, there is a strong academic, intellectual, and partly also Marxist opposition to the Chavists' Bolívar.

The first Venezuelan and Cuban Marxists deserve credit for detaching Bolívar from the autocratic tradition that developed after Páez and its maximal theorization by Vallenilla Lanz.[103] The criticism of the authoritarian Bolívar led to a new construction of the revolutionary Bolívar in the crisis of colonial society. It is indebted to a transnational Marxist historiography that reached from Venezuela and Cuba to other countries in Latin America and as far as the Soviet Union and the German Democratic Republic ("internationalism"). The myth of the revolutionary "leftist" Bolívar was connected with the criticism of Marx's article.[104]

The third historiographic line of development goes back to a leftist Marxist-Creole tradition in Venezuela itself and is connected with great names in the Venezuelan economy and social history: Eduardo Arcila Farías (1912–1996) and Federico Brito Figueroa

"Bolívar was no Communist."

(1921–2000) as well as Germán Carrera Damas (b. 1930). A few of these historians, such as Brito Figueroa and, *cum grano salis*, the German Latin-Americanist Max Zeuske (1927–2001), were labeled objectivist Marxist-Vallenists[105] because in the ideological horizon of the l960s and 1970s, they used the Marxist concept of dictatorship to explain the dictatorship of Bolívar, who believed that he could maintain Great Colombia in no other way.

In any case, it is certain that around 1990 there was a clearly defined "leftist" and international Bolívar with whom Marxists could agree, if they took any interest at all in a man and an aristocrat like Bolívar.[106]

Around 1990, the splitting of the "leftist Bolívar" into a rather more conservative "social-democratic Bolívar," who lent legitimacy to the Acción Democrática party in the Punto Fijo democracy, and a radical-esoteric "people's Bolívar" aroused little interest outside Venezuela. In contrast, the "leftist" social-revolutionary Bolívar who had an Afro-Venezuelan great-grandmother and who came closer to the Bolívar of the oral tradition, attracted a great deal of attention in the dynamic time of the neoliberal "adaptation" and the violent protests and subsequent massacre in Caracas known as the Caracazo (1989).

It is understandable that in all the ideological, mythological, and historiographic debates, the complicated real history of the wars for independence was not central. However, it leads to the discussion centered on Bolívar and a single version of the Independencia, not on the distinct traits of a "social revolution from below" in the wars from 1811 to 1821 (and far beyond). A history of the Independencia and the crises of the nineteenth century "without Bolívar" is nowhere to be found. Any kind of history with the Bolívar myth leads to an ideological-hermeneutic circle: whether good or ill is said about Bolívar, it always contributes to his fame. This is where another version, which might be called the transatlantic Bolívar-Humboldt myth, belongs.

CHAPTER III

Excursus: "Humboldt and Bolívar"— On a Conversation That May Never Have Taken Place

================

This excursus is a kind of textual archeology. Just as the archeologist excavates layer after layer of earth, we have to excavate the superimposed writings that have been produced by the Bolívar myth over the centuries. Finally, by way of an example, we will show first how the initiation of a mythical hero was consecrated by a more elevated figure—in this case, the "barón de Humboldt"—and second how the necessary textual authenticity was constructed.

The sole direct connection suggesting that Humboldt even noticed Bolívar before the beginning of the Independencia is a passage in an 1806 letter to Bonpland: "What do you think about Miranda? And the young Bolívar, will he be there? What companions! You'll see, this will turn out badly."[1] Humboldt was referring the expedition Francisco de Miranda undertook in 1806 to transform the Spanish colonial empire, by military means and with Haitian and secret British and American help, into a huge independent empire under the name of "Colombia" or "Hispano-Colombian Continent."[2] This attempt failed. But the reference to Bolívar in connection with Miranda (who is now once again celebrated as a hero and revolutionary) indicates that Humboldt saw both of them as belonging to the group that sought to establish by force a "white republic."

However, Humboldt was a reformer and not a revolutionary, or at least not a political revolutionary. As we have seen, he rejected certain groups in the Creole upper class with which he had personal

Bolívar and Humboldt in Paris.

contact. He alleged that they were "Jacobins" striving to create a "white republic," that is, an intensification of slavery and racism, by violent means. And he went even further: in the article "Colonies" (1803), he flatly condemned a revolution by the elites of Spanish America: "In this situation a confusion of inconceivable ideas and feelings is emerging, a general revolutionary tendency. But this is no more than a desire to expel the Europeans and afterward to fight among themselves."[3]

In the letter to Bonpland, Humboldt makes it clear that he saw both the "young Bolívar" and Miranda as belonging to the group of "revolutionaries" and "terrorist Jacobins" he rejected. The letter tells us no more than this. Humboldt says nothing about having met Bolívar, and consequently nothing about the content of any possible conversations with him.

A further clue might be found in the letters Bolívar and Humboldt exchanged. The best of several editions of the correspondence is that by Charles Minguet.[4] The two letters Bolívar wrote to Humboldt and the three that Humboldt wrote to Bolívar show one thing above all: their correspondence did not begin until 1821, after the victories won by the Bolívarian troops and the founding of the new state of Colombia. Bolívar's first letter to Humboldt begins with the salutation "Muy señor mío y respetable amigo" (My dear sir and honorable friend). He goes on: "Please accept the heartfelt memories of a man who had the honor to respect you before he met you, and to love you when he saw you in Paris and Rome."[5]

Here Bolívar says that he saw Humboldt, not that they spoke with each other. Had the two men actually long been "friends," they would have written to each other earlier. For this reason, the passage in Humboldt's letter in which he recalls the time of Bolívar's stay in Europe in 1804/5 is to be interpreted as mere politeness: "The friendship with which the General [Bolívar] saw fit to honor me after my return from Mexico, at a time when we were speaking out on behalf of the independence and freedom of the new continent."[6] Basically, these are diplomatic courtesies, especially on Humboldt's part. There is nothing new here regarding a meeting and the content of personal conversations between the two men.

The passage in the repeatedly quoted letter written by Vicente Rocafuerte (1783–1847) to Humboldt in 1824 should also be seen as amiable but empty phrases: "Bolívar ... was honored with your affectionate friendship in Paris [1804] and benefited in certain ways from your enormously wise advice; [he] was at that time so rash, so nonchalant, so inconsistent."[7]

The third written reference to a direct meeting between Humboldt and Bolívar seems to be the clearest and most informative. It communicates the elderly Humboldt's regret for his earlier assessment of Bolívar. The text is long:

After my return from America—Humboldt then told his visitor [Daniel Florencio O'Leary]—I had much intercourse with Bolívar. His lively conversation, his love of peoples' liberation, his fascination with the constructions of his brilliant imagination led me to see in him a dreamer. I never thought he would become the leader of an American crusade.

Since I had thoroughly explored the Spanish colonies and acquired a feeling for the political situation in many of them, I could judge more accurately than Bolívar, who knew only Venezuela. During my stay in America I never encountered dissatisfaction.[8] But I did see that if there was also no great love for the Spaniards, at least people had accepted the existing regime. I understood only later, when the fighting began, that people had concealed the truth from me, and that instead of love there were deep and long established feelings of hate that broke out amid a whirl of acts of retaliation and revenge. But what surprised me most was Bolívar's brilliant career shortly after we separated, when I left Paris in 1805 and went to Italy. The actions, the talents, and the fame of this great man led me to recall his moments of enthusiasm when we shared our wishes for the liberation of Spanish America.[9] I acknowledge that I was mistaken at that time, when I thought him an immature person incapable of a fruitful enterprise such as he then vaingloriously conceived. Because of my studies in the various crises of American society, it seemed to me that if a man could ever appear with the ability to undertake a revolution, it would be in New Granada (then called Colombia),[10] where manifestations had already appeared at the end of the last century and whose tendencies were not unknown to me. My colleague Bonpland was shrewder than I. From the outset, he had formed a more positive judgment of Bolívar and encouraged him in my presence. I remember that one morning he (Bonpland) wrote to me that Bolívar had told him about plans that filled him with enthusiasm for Venezuela's independence, and it would not be surprising if he were able to carry them out; he said that he (Bonpland) had a very favorable view of his young friend. At that time it seemed to me that Bonpland was also talking nonsense. He was not mistaken, but I was. I was very late in seeing my error regarding this great man, whose acts I admire, whose friendship became an honor to me, and who is famous throughout the world.

This quotation is taken from a book by Günter Kahle, a historian of Latin America in Cologne.[11] Eleven years before Kahle, the Leipzig historian Manfred Kossok had already quoted in full this allegedly authentic statement of Humboldt's, which was supposed to have been transmitted via Daniel Florencio O'Leary.[12] Kossok omitted only the comment inserted between dashes, "Humboldt then told his visitor."[13] Both Kossok and Kahle give an article by Hanns Heiman (1959) as the source of the quotation.[14] So far, so good.

In earlier studies on the subject of Humboldt and Bolívar, I myself assumed this quotation was authentic.[15] Only in November 2010 did it occur to me to look beyond the authorities I had relied on and to compare the passage with the one from 1853, either Humboldt's or O'Leary's. An archeology of the textual layers. First I saw that Hanns Heiman quoted no source. In such cases it usually helps to consult one of the famous Humboldt scholars: Kurt-R. Biermann or Hanno Beck. In this matter, both were relevant. Biermann[16] adopts the "Memory of Humboldt" transmitted by O'Leary, viz., from "a conversation with General O'Leary" that he proves by reference to Hanno Beck.[17] Beck in turn cites Cornelio Hispano, *El libro de oro de Bolívar* (*The Golden Book of Bolívar*, 1925).

Cornelio Hispano's name set off alarms for me. It is the pseudonym of the Colombian intellectual Ismael López (1880–1962). This pseudonym is a program: "Cornelio" is derived from the old Roman family of the Cornelians, and "Hispano" means, of course, "the Spaniard." This is the program of Colombia's conservative elite, concentrated in Bogotá, to establish an educational canon based on European Hispanism, which was in turn believed to be rooted in ancient Rome. What was supposed to matter was not, for instance, the living culture of South American peasants, Indios, ex-slaves, and the urban population of the immediate present and environment but rather the conventional wisdom of the European elites and, as much as possible, the elites of the Catholic and "Roman" part of old Europe, passing from Italy and Greece by way of France to Spain—and thus to Latin America as well.

At the outset, in the 1850s, Latin America had taken its models essentially from France and Italy. After 1898, under the concept of "Latin," a renaissance of *hispanidad* (a cultural orientation toward traditional Spain) began. Cornelio Hispano's hispanistic plan sought to achieve a Spanish language whose form and sound would be, as far as possible, more classical than the Spanish (or, rather, the Castilian) of Spain itself.

In the edition of the *Libro de oro de Bolívar* brought out by a Chavist publishing house, we can quite easily find the passage to which Kahle, Kossok, and Heiman, as well as Beck and Biermann, refer.[18] Hispano gives the whole passage that everyone cites, but through the little word *dijo* ("he said") in the first sentence of the passage (a word Kossok omitted) he gives away the fact that he or Arístides Rojas, to whom Hispano himself refers, invented or "imagined" the passage.

First, Hispano introduces the scene in 1853, when O'Leary is supposed to have been with Humboldt: "Twenty-three years after Bolívar's death, during a meeting that General O'Leary, as the Liberator's friend and adjutant, had with Humboldt at the behest of Lord Clarendon in order to discuss certain subjects in connection with the opening of the interoceanic canal through the isthmus of Darién [later the Panama Canal], Humboldt spoke, immediately after he had discussed this matter with his conversation partner, about Spanish America and Bolívar: …"[19]

In Hispano's account, this is a description and not a quotation. Only after the colon does the citation and ablation of the whole passage cited above follow, between quotation marks, as it is taken over by Heiman, Kahle, Kossok, and Beck (Biermann does not quote it in full). In Hispano, the first sentence reads: "I had much intercourse with him after my return from America, he said, at the end of 1804."[20] Hispano also adds a footnote (note 4) in which he gives the source: "Centenario de Bolívar. Bogotá, 1883" (edited by Alberto Urdaneta).[21] This book contains texts by Arístides Rojas, which Hispano adopts.

Charles Minguet (1925–1998), probably the foremost expert on Humboldt, cites the passage we are concerned with here. However, Minguet does not, like Hanno Beck, give Cornelio Hispano as the source, but rather the document "Testimonio del general D. F. O'Leary, 1853" (Testimony of General D. F. O'Leary, 1853), and supports this by reference to "A. Rojas, *Humboldtianas*, Buenos Aires-Caracas, 1941 [in fact, 1942], 2 vols., tomo III [in fact, vol. 2], págs. 179–180 [in fact, pp. 179–181]."[22] Minguet gives the first sentence this way: "Traté mucho a éste [Bolívar] después de mi regreso de América, a fines de 1804 [decía Humboldt a O'Leary]" (I had much intercourse with him [Bolívar] after my return from America, toward the end of 1804 [said Humboldt to O'Leary]).[23]

All the various quotations and text passages go back to Arístides Rojas, who did not transcribe the source text but instead actually invented it, in order to lend authenticity to the myth. The archeology of the text thus arrives at the lowest stratum on which all the others are based. It must now be shown how the construction was built and who, in addition to Arístides
Rojas, was the builder.

Arístides Rojas, the pioneer of costrumbrism and one of the most important historians who worked under Antonio Guzmán Blanco,[24] whose tomb is now in the Panteón Nacional in Caracas, never actually met Humboldt. But he collected all the information he could find about the German naturalist in Venezuela and wrote it down. In accord with his method of transcribing oral tradition in writing, he had transcribed the long original 1853 passage about Humboldt's memories of Bolívar in 1804 and transformed it into literature. Rojas did not merely repeat what he might have been told was "O'Leary's testimony." Instead, he created his own source, so to speak. It is possible that crucial oral information came from O'Leary's son Simón B., who was living in Caracas in the

1870s in order to sell his father's *Memoirs* to the Venezuelan government.

In volume 2 of his *Humboldtianas*, Rojas puts the passage between quotation marks and names his source in a footnote: "Extracto sacado de las Notas de Viaje del General O'Leary" (Extract taken from General O'Leary's Travel Notes).[25] What is remarkable about this is that there are no "travel notes" of Leary's regarding a trip to Berlin in 1853. They simply do not exist. In 1853, Daniel F. O'Leary made no trip to Berlin. Where Rojas writes "Extracto sacado," he means that he "created" or "imagined" them—to put it more clearly, *invented*; more bluntly, *forged*; or more scientifically, *constructed* them. That means that Rojas collected, harmonized, and canonized recollections that were circulating orally and may have already been printed here and there in various versions. What these recollections actually contained, no one knows. The same thing happened with Bible texts, though obviously on another scale and in other periods. Since a mere collection of the contents of conversations and conjectures was then not considered scientific, Rojas invented O'Leary's "Notas de Viaje." Moreover, he imagined O'Leary's visit to Berlin in 1853. There is no evidence in any of the biographies of O'Leary that proves that he traveled to Berlin in 1853 or met there with Humboldt. In his actual memorandum book, *Detached Recollections*, which only goes up to 1840, O'Leary mentions, under the laconic title "Bolívar in Paris" (1804), Bolívar's romantic adventures and party anecdotes but not a meeting between Bolívar and Humboldt: "When at Paris B[olívar] paid much attention to a young lady with whom Prince Eugene Beauharnais was also enamoured. Being one day at an entertainment at which the lady and the Prince assisted, the former asked the latter what animal did B[olívar] resemble. To a sparrow was the reply. The name of the bird in French [*moineau*—MZ] sounds like that of monkey in Spanish [*mono*—MZ], and this latter was the signification which B[olívar] gave to the word, at which he immediately took offence and in anger said to the Prince, 'and you are like a crow.' It was not until after many assurances that the Prince meant no offence and that the true sense of the word was explained to him that he became appeased."[26]

Charles Minguet suggests that key statements in the putative conversation—in other versions, it is referred to as a letter—that Humboldt is supposed to have had with O'Leary existed long before 1853 or were circulating orally in the form of recollections and discussions. In the introduction to the famous first Bolívar archive put together by Javier Francisco Yanes and Cristóbal Mendoza (Colección Yanes-Mendoza, 1826–1829), which Minguet cites and which was published in the first volume of the *Escritos del Libertador*, we already read, regarding Bolívar's trip to Europe between 1804 and 1806: "One of his encounters during this trip was the one with Baron von Humboldt, who had visited us [!—MZ] a few years earlier, and when he [Bolívar] asked him [Humboldt] what he thought of his project [of Independencia—MZ], that wise man replied: 'I think that the country is ready, but I don't see the man who could carry out this project.'… And he [Humboldt] had him right in front of him, but he [Bolívar] himself did not yet recognize himself."[27]

That could have been written by Cristóbal Mendoza, who as an eighteen-year-old might have met or seen Humboldt during the latter's stay in Caracas or in the valleys of the Aragua. In any case, in the 1820s, Javier Francisco Yanes and Cristóbal Mendoza did socialize with O'Leary, who had obviously already begun writing down his *Narración*, his version of the history of Independencia (which is essentially the Bolívarians' version). In the introduction to the *Colección*, Yanes and Mendoza quote from O'Leary's text, which had not yet been published. The *Colección* appeared between 1826 and 1829—but O'Leary is supposed to have met Humboldt in Berlin only in 1853! Thus we encounter many incongruences and contradictions—here, historical research is like detective work.

In 1865, Felipe Larrazábal, an earlier biographer of Bolívar, still clings to the version given in the *Colección*, though he appears more scholarly and establishes a direct connection with French culture, which in his time was fashionable among the elites of Venezuela: "Bolívar spoke French perfectly and fluently, and in it he found the concepts suitable for expressing his ideas concerning the indignity of colonial life and the freedom and greatness of

America's future destiny; and the Baron [Humboldt] replied: "That is so, Sir, and I believe that your country is already capable of receiving emancipation, but who is the man who can undertake this great task? The man was standing before him, but he didn't realize it. Bolívar could have answered him [in Latin]: I am he, I who am speaking with you. ..."[28]

With the quotations of Felipe Larrazábal and especially of Cristobál Mendoza (and Yanes), the circle of constructions is complete. Cristóbal Mendoza belonged to the old Creole oligarchy that before 1810 dominated *de facto* Caracas and Bourbon Venezuela and, with the rebellion of April 19, 1810, sought to found *de jure* a more or less autonomous state. Mendoza was also one of the three alternating presidents of the Confederación Americana de Venezuela founded in 1811. In 1812, when the political project of autonomy and federation had already failed and the age of civil and caudillo wars began, most members of the oligarchy had gone over to the loyalist camp again. Mendoza himself—and after 1821, this predestined him to speak for all his surviving friends from the oligarchy—had remained in the small group of militarily radical Bolívarianos until 1814. As we have seen, he had arranged for Bolívar to receive the title of "Libertador" in the framework of a general cult of the homeland. In the battle of Carabobo (1821), Bolívar's and Páez's patriot troops rather surprisingly defeated the royal troops led by Francisco Tomás Morales. Immediately thereafter began the reconstruction of the old exploitative order and slavery that I call as a whole the "colonial extraction machinery."[29] This was justified by constructing a temporally and spatially fixed movement that was henceforth called Independencia and firmly attached to the victorious General Bolívar.

Because of Bolívar's policy of alliances with other movements, the surviving Caracas oligarchy still considered him one of their own, even when the Libertador reappeared in 1821 surrounded by black soldiers and colored Llanero officers. The one and only Independencia was subdivided with Roman numerals and populated with white upper-class Creoles. In the framework of this oligarchic interpretation of "Independencia with Bolívar," all those who had met and spoken with Humboldt in 1800 could now claim to have been progressive revolutionaries at that point, because they had spoken with the author (Humboldt) who published the *Relation historique* in 1827,[30] in which he justified Independencia in an almost scientific way. Arístides Rojas found a very apt linguistic form for the significant content of this construction: "Around that time [when Humboldt was in Venezuela and Caracas—MZ], all men began to awaken from the revolution as progressive spirits."[31] In retrospect, the oligarchic elites relied on Humboldt as an authority because in reality they had never been revolutionaries; at first, they sought only to achieve autonomy, and between 1814 and 1821, they had faithfully served the Spanish king again and sworn loyalty to him in writing and in elaborate rituals.

Mendoza and his collaborators set rebellions and revolts that moved in stages toward the freedom movement against the background of the spatiotemporal construct of Independencia. They appropriated precursors ("pre-heroes") such as Juan Francisco de León (1699–1752), Manuel Gual (1754–1800), José María España (1761–1799), and Francisco de Miranda. Then on April 19, 1810, the triggering event—the "Caracas revolution"—was supposed to have come, and Caracas and the oligarchy surviving there were already called the *cuna de la Independencia* (the cradle of independence).

Cristóbal Mendoza managed all this by means of a relatively simple device. He interwove two explosive linguistic, discursive, rumor-based, devotional, and anecdotal complexes—the raw material of great myths that were then already skillfully playing with written and oral *memoria*. First, he took the memories of Humboldt's stay in Venezuela that persisted in oral and private written form in municipal offices and on the mantuanos' slave-holding haciendas. To these, he added the discussions concerning the works of Humboldt that had been in circulation since 1827, in particular the *Relation historique*. Mendoza combined these two strands to create a "single Independencia with Bolívar." This seemed plausible and posed no problem for the intellectual elite that controlled the new journalistic media.

The second operation was a masterpiece from which sparks truly flew. Mendoza hot-wired the Humboldt discourse to the oral and visual discursive complex of the already circulating first Bolívar cult. Sparks of charismatic energy were immediately emitted. A historic core of justification for all the Bolívar myths resulted, a kind of myth-battery that has been constantly further elaborated during the intervening two hundred years and that made it possible to dynamically ground the nation whose first name is Venezuela and to re-legitimate it repeatedly down to the present day. Not even the living Bolívar, in his last years, or the recently deceased Libertador and the betrayal of him in 1830 could halt or prevent this dynamic of myths. And historians who unmasked the myths as "false ideology" fared no better.

Cristóbal Mendoza—and in his wake, whole troops of writers, including his direct descendent Cristóbal L. Mendoza—succeeded in further developing two myths that have since changed the world: the myth of the (political) "revolutionary Humboldt" and the myth of the "genius Bolívar" who had been first awakened by his conversation with Alexander von Humboldt in 1804. In the interim, the initiation by Humboldt has become the most important part of the Bolívar myth, which has now taken on world-wide dimensions. Even today, in every publication or exhibit about "Humboldt and Bolívar," "Venezuela and Germany," or even "Latin America and Germany," the two myths are invoked and mutually reinforce one another. Between 1826 and 1959, so many textual layers were produced by this transatlantic back-and-forth that they could not be sorted out even by experienced historians of Latin America. And Humboldt experts followed the Latin America specialists.

However, the historians of the generation of the 1930s whom we have quoted (in particular, Manfred Kossok and Günter Kahle) were not exposed, as was the generation of historians who held university chairs around 1990, to the extreme pressure exerted by the globally operating media industry that henceforth made use of the myths and adapted them to its virtual world. Around 1990, in writing their more or less completed works, my teachers Manfred Kossok and Günter Kahle had no access to ways of deconstructing these modern myths. They would have had to give up the "objective" knowledge that was for them the firm foundation of their science. In the 1990s, all younger historians, including myself, confronted different problems. Most of them abandoned belief in a reality of history and devoted themselves to a history of culture and media in which one paradigm change followed another. Reason for concern then arises when scholarly works are caught up in the virtual world of the media and create the impression that "reality" can be grasped only through that world.

A minority of social historians concentrated on the microscopic investigation of historical figures in the mode of "life histories," doing intensive research in archives and other forms of *memoria*—which leads to the danger of adopting the myth uncritically and considering it alone to be true. Research on slavery and the postcolonialism debate allowed me to maintain my conviction that there is a reality of history—populated by individuals and their self-testimonies—and at the same time to situate it critically in relation to the cults and myths that have been handed down to us and that surround historical persons.

Postscript, April 2012

The archeology of the text continues to provide exciting discoveries. In April 2012, Professor Alberto Gómez Gutiérrez, a well-known Humboldt scholar at the Universidad Javeriana in Bogotá, wrote to tell me that he had found a Humboldt manuscript in the Biblioteca Luis Angel Arango (wrongly classified as a letter from Humboldt to Bolivar). The manuscript reads:

> It is with the greatest pleasure that I shall have the honor of receiving General O'Leary on Thursday [underlined in the original—MZ] the 22nd, at 1:00 p.m., in order to thank him for generously sending me a letter written by the clever Mr. Pentland and to refresh with him memories of my illustrious friend General Bolívar. I [trust], Sir, that the day and the hour will be convenient for you, deeply regretting that I cannot sooner

> enjoy your friendly and instructive conversation. ...
> I beg you, General, to accept my highest regards, along with which I have the honor of being your very humble and very obedient servant[.]
>
> —Alexander von Humboldt[32]

Unfortunately, the manuscript does not indicate the year. But it might very well refer to April 22, 1853 (which was a Thursday). Then O'Leary would have been at Humboldt's residence in Berlin, even though this is not mentioned in any biography. Alberto Gómez has also drawn to my attention the correspondence between O'Leary and his wife Soledad Soublette, which makes no reference to a visit to Berlin and Humboldt in 1853 but does show, at least, that O'Leary could have been in Berlin between his visits to Rome (April 1, 1853) and Paris (April 29 and 30, 1853).[33]

INSTEAD OF A CONCLUSION

The "Chavist Bolívar"

Ever since its construction, the Humboldt myth, as a submyth of the Bolívar myth, has remained alive among intellectuals and in the middle classes in Venezuela.[1] The president of Venezuela, Hugo Chávez (b. 1954), grew up in a poor family in the Llano state of Barinas. During the first twenty years of his life, Chávez was influenced, on the one hand, by the noncanonical version of the "people's Bolívar" myth and, on the other hand, by the conservative, rather positivistic Bolívar myth of the Punto Fijo democracy.[2] Moreover, he had heard of Humboldt, because he and many Chavists also grew up reading books like Cornelio Hispano's *El libro de oro de Bolívar*. For them, the "1804 meeting" was the beginning of a close friendship between Humboldt and Bolívar.

During the various stages of his political life— during officer school, the military conspiracy, the officers' rebellion of 1992, the phase of orientation and election campaigning up to 1998, and the various steps leading to power—Chávez and the inner core of Chavistas have always been guided by two versions of the Bolívar myth, the plebeian-mulatto version and the conservative-positivist-nationalist version. It is obvious that in the process, new life was also breathed into the liberal version of the Independencia myth.[3] But the legitimation of the Cuban revolution, which saw one of its roots in the battle fought by the revolutionary Bolívar, may also have played a role: Che Guevara is said to have vehemently defended Bolívar against Marx.

The Marxist and internationalist wing of Chavism, which has little interest in being associated with Bolívar, has nonetheless subordinated itself to the concept of the "Chavist Bolívar." Thus new dimensions of Bolívarism have emerged. The Libertador remains the number one historical hero of Venezuela. Hugo Chávez has always exploited all the possible forms of the Bolívar cult: patriarchalism (in the form of *oficialismo*, one of the best targets for the intellectual opposition's attacks), quoting Bolívar as the "last word," and continental nationalism. Not letting Bolívar's famous oath (1805) rest until the yoke of oppression has been thrown off is only one manifestation of the myth,[4] but it is an important one that was especially present in a few versions of the Humboldt myth.

At the beginning of his term of office, when he was putting together his political party, Chávez was even tempted to accept groups of supporters organized into Circulos Bolívarianos. But he distanced himself from them relatively quickly, because the name Bolívar was not to be used solely for a party or group. The program of the "Bolívarist process" foresees a new notion of history in which the Afro-Venezuelan and rural history of the country play a prominent role connected above all with figures like the first "anti-imperialist," Francisco de Miranda, Ezequiel Zamora, and a multitude of local heroes like Maisanta who have survived in oral traditions. Although there are also new kinds of memories, such as the famous *arból de las tres raíces*—the tree with three roots, symbolizing Simón Bolívar, Simón Rodríguez, and Ezequiel Zamora[5]—the Chavistas have not long held onto them or to other archives and visualizations. They immediately claimed the "Bolívar" brand for everything: for the state (República Bolívariana de Venezuela), the new constitution (Constitución Bolívariana), the most important initial social mission (Misión Bolívar), and a series of foreign and Latin American projects.

All this somewhat naive-seeming Bolívarism and nationalism at the beginning of the Chávez period can still be explained by the fact that Chávez had to start out from what was known to the general population in whose name he governed (and that up to the present has always voted for him by majorities of about 60 percent). The opposition conspiring against Chávez in 2002 had put at the top of its list of priorities the abolition of this new republic in the name of Bolívar, and it would certainly have gladly returned to the conservative Bolívar civil religion of the years preceding 1960 (or would have thrown Bolívar on the rubbish heap of history, as many Chávez's current opponents seem inclined to do).

In the meantime, the more prudent opposition limits itself to criticizing the Chavist "social-revolutionary Bolívar"[6] and is concerned with the "people's Bolívar"—never before have Venezuela's publishers, journalists, scholars, and university professors been so intensively occupied with the history of their own people. This history has become itself a legitimating force. The critics attack, often with justification, the still pervasive conservative-nationalist Bolívar. Then they broaden their rejection to the social Bolívar, with the aim of discrediting the Chavists' main source of legitimation.

In a sense, the Chavist Bolívar is the answer to two centuries of the Bolívar myth from above that was dictated to people in repeatedly appearing archives and academic discourses. Its spokesman, who sees himself as the leader of the "Bolivarian process," is using the material of conservative Bolívar exegesis in order to create a new Bolívar myth. The latter already goes beyond all earlier Bolívar myths in the quantity of printed paper it has generated. As can be seen in military reviews, parades, and state receptions, there is also a new Bolívar cult.

The "Bolivarian process" led by Hugo Chávez sees itself as a profound sociopolitical transformation in the tradition of earlier battles. This is shown in the reorientation of the political Bolívar cult toward a more social Bolívar myth and a continent-wide Bolívar cult. And it is shown in its differentiation: almost all Chavist social programs, the *misiones*, bear the names of Bolívar's contemporaries or companions in arms. Even José Antonio Páez is memorialized with the Vuelvan Caras—a legendary order given by the cavalry commander who after a feigned retreat told his Llaneros to "look backward" and then attacked the pursuers. Sucre (Antonio José de Sucre), Robinson (Simón Rodríguez) and Hipólita (Bolívar's ex-slave and nurse) are all eponyms. The Misión Zamora land reform represents a separate area—hardly anyone had yet sought to connect Bolívar or his companions in arms with agrarian reform.[7]

Continental Bolívarism has offered new perspectives with the South American defense alliance ALBA (Alternativa Bolívariana para las Américas) and the South American banking, commercial, and communications organizations Bancosur, Mercosur, and Telesur, as well as many other initiatives in practical policy and global foreign policy. Here the efforts made by Bolívar in his own time and those of contemporary Bolívarism quite clearly correspond to one another. However, it is striking that only a few of the projects are really related to Bolívar. That connection is opposed by Venezuela's partners, especially the South American superpowers Brazil and Argentina. In this respect, the connective "south" is more important.[8] In my opinion, as a movement, Bolívarism seeks not only leadership by the military and a presidency oriented toward personalism but also changes in structures and conditions (which are, however, increasingly threatened by bureaucracy, corruption, and insecurity).[9]

All this greatly concerns the work of historians and social scientists. However, periods of political transformation and polarization have never been times of contemplative historical research. Nevertheless, there has been a series of good historical investigations, particularly in the areas of the resistance to colonialism and slavery, the agrarian rebellions, and the political battles of the nineteenth and twentieth centuries, as well as in regional history and historical anthropology. But they have hardly been extended to the history of the colonial structures long before Independencia, on the one hand, or to the history of myths, on the other hand. In particular, there is a lack of connection between research and the political program of the "Bolívarian process," because most academics are on the side of the opposition. The traditional conservative Bolívarianos, some of whom are also supporters of the intellectual Bolívar-Humboldt submyth, were for the most part opposed from the outset to Chávez and his social-revolutionary Bolívar.[10]

Frédérique Langue writes: "The interest in the current rewriting of history by this same President Chávez is rooted in the fact that Bolívar is no longer supposed to be the white aristocrat (mantuano) or defender of order that he had been even for certain European authors [a reference to Marx—MZ]. According to various defenders of the [Chávez] regime, he was transformed into a mestizo or, more precisely, into a zambo."[11]

The observer is struck by the way the Bolívar myth has grown, since the 1980s and especially since 1999, in the direction of a "social-revolutionary Bolívar" within Venezuela and a Bolívar reinterpreted as a strategic, continental thinker for foreign consumption. But the new historical conception did not lead to a critical historicization of Bolívar and a revision of the historical notion of the one and only Independencia. Instead, the connections, images, words, devotions, and celebrations became even more gigantic, as in a conservative cult that was already of enormous dimensions in 1998. To that extent, we still cannot say, after more than a decade of "Bolívarian Chavism" or "Chavist Bolívarism," whether we are seeing only a new stage in the Bolívar myth or whether instead the "Bolívarian process" is eventually going to lead to a profound transformation. Similarly, we have no definitive answer to the question whether we are witnessing an actual social revolution or only one of many changes of elites accompanied by an exchange of clienteles.

All of Venezuela's elites, including that of the late José Antonio Páez, have sought to speak Bolívar's language and to incorporate his myth into a cult of the nation with the forename of Venezuela. However, such a strong nationalist continuity is rather puzzling in the case of a movement that since 2005 has also dedicated itself increasingly to a "socialism of the twenty-first century." But the project has great staying power.[12] That much is clear after more than a decade of the "Bolívarian process" inside and outside the Bolívarian Republic. Moreover, the Bolívar myth is not only ambivalent but also polysemous. Perhaps the reasons for the longevity of Bolívarian Chavism and the Chavist Bolívar lie not so much in the discursive autonomy of myths, rituals, words, and images but rather in the extreme persistence of Venezuela's social and structural problems—and in the power of the popular notion that only one of the Creole elite revolutionaries dared, for whatever reasons, to attack the bases of social injustice—slavery and large landed estates—at least discursively.

Marc Saint-Upéry describes a carnival in Rio in 2006: "The famous samba school, Vila Isabel, proudly surrounds a splendid carriage on which an impressive figure rises skyward, twelve meters high, garbed in a steel-blue greatcoat adorned with gilt epaulets and trim. The Napoleonic uniform, the mutton-chops in the Empire style, the tricolor yellow-gold-red [the national colors of Venezuela and Colombia—MZ] allow no doubt: Simón Bolívar is the historical figure leading the procession, the man who freed a third of the continent from the Spanish yoke and dreamed of one day seeing it a confederation characterized by freedom and solidarity. Around him the samba dancers move in a frenetic rhythm, singing in 'Portuñol' [a mixture of Portuguese and Spanish—MZ]: I'm crazy about you, America. The figure of Bolívar is accompanied by images of San Martín, his Argentine counterpart, the Brazilian general Abreu Lima, who fought in Bolívar's army, Tiradentes, the heroic forerunner of Brazilian independence, Ernesto 'Che' Guevara, Salvador Allende, and half a dozen other political and literary celebrities such as the Cuban José Martí, the Chilean Pablo Neruda, and the bossa nova poet Vinicius de Morães. It is the heterogeneous pantheon of the continental left."[13]

In the meantime, the Vila Isabel samba school has gone bankrupt, but this beautiful version of a Bolívar myth going worldwide in samba rhythm—with elements of the conservative myth, it is true, but in the framework of a popular Bolívar cult as part of the carnival in Rio—is still very exciting.

NOTES

Introduction

1. Ramón Gutiérrez and Rodrigo Gutiérrez Viñuales, *América y España: Imágenes para una historia; Independencia e identidad 1805–1925* (Madrid, 2006).
2. Simón Bolívar's archive in the true sense consists of 208 bound volumes that were initially stored in the Casa Natal del Libertador (the house where the Liberator was born) in Caracas and are now in the Archivo Histórico Nacional. During Bolívar's lifetime and especially after his death in 1830, the archive, still in leather boxes and crates, was assembled and preserved by his adjutant, the Irish soldier Daniel Florencio O'Leary (1801–1854). After Bolívar's death, O'Leary, who is also called "Bolívar's evangelist," saw his life's work as publishing these sources and documents. See *Memorias del General O'Leary, publicadas por su hijo Simón B. o'Leary, por orden del gobierno de Venezuela y bajo los auspicios de su presidente General Guzmán Blanco, Ilustre Americano, Regenerador de la República*, 32 vols. (Caracas, 1882; repr. as *Memorias del General O'Leary, edición facsimilar del original de la primera edición, con motivo de la celebración del Sesquicentenario de la Muerte de Simón Bolívar, Padre de la Patria*, 34 vols. Caracas: Ministerio de la Defensa, 1981); see also Daniel O'Leary: *Actividades diplomáticas del general Daniel Florencio O'Leary en Europa, años de 1834 a 1839: cartas al general Carlos Soublette, vicepresidente de la República* (Caracas, 1939). Further archives are Cristóbal Mendoza and Javier Francisco Yanes, *Colección de documentos relativos a la vida pública del Libertador de Colombia y del Perú, Simón Bolívar para servir a la historia de Independencia de Sur América*, 21 vols. (Caracas, 1826–1829; appendix, 1833) (hereafter cited as "Colección Yanes-Mendoza"); Felipe Larrazábal, *Correspondencia General del Libertador Simón Bolívar: Enriquecida con la inserción de los manifiestos, mensages, exposiciones, proclamas & &, publicadas por el Heroe Colombiano desde 1810 hasta 1830 (precede á esta colección interesante la vida de Bolívar)*, 2 vols. (New York, 1865); José Félix Blanco and Ramón Azpurúa (eds.), *Documentos para la historia de la vida pública del Libertador*, 16 vols. (Caracas, 1978); Simón Bolívar, *Cartas del Libertador corregidas conforme a los originales*, ed. Vicente Lecuna, 10 vols. (Caracas, 1929–1939; vol. 11, 1954); Sociedad Bolivariana de Venezuela (ed.), *Bolívar, Escritos del Liber-*

tador, 28 vols. (Caracas, 1964–1988) (hereafter cited as *Escritos del Libertador*); Simón Bolívar, *Obras Completas*, 3 vols. (Caracas, 1982); Comité Regional Bicentenario del Natalicio del Libertador (Estado Miranda) (ed.), *Decretos del Libertador*, 3 vols. (Los Teques: Biblioteca de Autores y Temas Mirandinos, 1983); see German: Hans-Joachim König (ed.), *Simón Bolívar: Reden und Schriften zu Politik, Wirtschaft und Gesellschaft; Mit einem Vorwort v. B. Betancourt* (Hamburg, 1984); see also "Contribución a la Bibliografía de los Escritos del Libertador," in *Escritos del Libertador*, vol. 1, pp. 61–290; Pedro Grases, "El archivo del Libertador," in idem, *El Archivo de Bolívar. Manuscritos y ediciones* (Caracas, 1978), pp. 15–62.
3. Rafael Pineda: *Las estatuas de Simón Bolívar en el mundo* (Caracas, 1983).
4. Napoleón Franceschi González, "Simón Bolívar: El culto al héroe máximo," *Anuario de Estudios Bolivarianos* 5, no. 5 (1996): 133–185.
5. Germán Carrera Damas, *El culto a Bolívar: esbozo para un estudio de la historia de las ideas en Venezuela* (Caracas, 1969) (and numerous later editions); the same goes for John Lynch, "The Cult of Bolívar," *Simón Bolívar: A Life* (New Haven, 2006), pp. 299–304.
6. Because empirical investigations of the Bolívar cult are lacking, the present work concentrates on the real person Bolívar and on the structural conditions of the emergence of the myth and a few of its dimensions.
7. James E. Sanders, "Atlantic Republicanism in Nineteenth-Century Colombia: Spanish America's Challenge to the Contours of Atlantic History," *Journal of World History* 20, no. 1 (2009): 131–150.
8. A not very hierarchical, syncretic religion communicated chiefly through "mediums" who work with trances. The core of the religion is the sacred history of the Indio princess María Lionza, who was protected by various *cortes* (courts) but was nevertheless transformed into an enormous green-eyed serpent and then carried away. The *cortes* provide everyday communication with María Lionza. With the *cortes*, every believer is given the option of putting together his own altar consisting of various deceased people—heroes, presidents, or film stars—and even entirely new courts, e.g., a *corte de los presidentes* consisting mainly of deceased presidents not only of Venezuela but might include, in addition to Bolívar, José Antonio Páez, Joseph Stalin, John F. Kennedy, and perhaps Juan Vicente Gómez. See María Lionza Pollak-Eltz, *Mito y culto venezolano* (Caracas, 1985); María Lionza Pollak-Eltz, "The Worship of Historical Personalities in the Cult of María Lionza in Venezuela," in *Anales del Caribe: Centro de*

Estudios del Caribe 19–20 (Havana, 1999/2000), pp. 187–191; Edmundo Bracho, *María Lionza en Venezuela* (Caracas, 2004).

9. Antonio López Ortega (ed.), *Atlas de Tradiciones Venezolanas* (Bogotá, 2005); Michael Zeuske, " 'Kommentare im Falsett': Medien, Nachrichten und Revolution am Beispiel der Independencia Venezuelas," *Comparativ*, fasc. 3 (1991): 54–68. One of the first textualizations is represented by the memoirs of José Antonio Páez; see José Antonio Páez, "Capítulo I, 1790–1809," in *Autobiografía del general José Antonio Páez*, 2 vols. (Bogotá, 1987) (facsimile of the original). On the survival of the oral tradition and its peculiar textual form (many are texts of Corridos and Joropos) as legends of famous deeds and heroes; see Antonio José Torrealba Osto, *Diario de un Llanero*, ed. with a study by E. Colmenares del Valle, 6 vols. (Caracas, 1987). The remarkable life history of the Llanero Antonio José Torrealba Osto (1883–1949) tells us a few things about the oral Cimarrón culture of the Llanos. Torrealba was "nieto de otomaca pura" (grandson of a pure Otomake) and the son of an Otomake's daughter and a white Creole father. He is thought to have been the most important source for Rómulo Gallegos when the latter was collecting the material for his novel *Doña Bárbara* in 1927.

10. Ana Cecilia Ojeda Avellaneda, *El mito Bolivariano en la literatura latinoamericana: Aproximaciones* (Bucaramanga, 2002); Christopher Conway, *The Cult of Bolívar in Latin American Literature* (Gainesville, FL, 2003); Domingo Irwin and Luis Butto, "The Literature behind Venezuelan Bolívarism," *Military Review* 86, no. 2 (2006): 82–87.

11. Germán Carrera Damas, *El culto a Bolívar: esbozo para un estudio de la historia de las ideas en Venezuela* (Caracas, 1969); John Chasteen, "Simón Bolívar: Man and Myth," in Samuel Brunk and Ben Fallaw (eds.), *Heroes and Hero Cults in Latin America* (Austin, TX, 2006), pp. 21–39; John V. Lombardi, "Epilogue: History and Our Heroes—The Bolívar Legend" and "Beginning to Read about Bolívar," in *Simón Bolívar: Essays on the Life and Legacy of the Liberator*, ed. David Bushnell and Lester D. Langley (Lanham, MD, 2008), pp. 159–191; see also Rebecca Earle " 'Padres de la Patria' and the Ancestral Past: Commemorations of Independence in Nineteenth Century Spanish America," *Journal of Latin American Studies* 34, no. 4 (2002): 775–806; idem, " 'Sobre Heroes y Tumbas': National Symbols in Nineteenth Century Spanish America," *Hispanic-American Historical Review* 85, no. 2 (2005): 375–416; Tomás Straka, "Venezuela: Bolívarismo, socialismo y democracia; La historia como debate político (1939–1999)," *Tiempos de América: Re-*

vista de Historia, Cultura y Territorio, no. 16 (1990): 63–83.
12. Yolanda Salas de Lecuna, *Bolívar y la historia en la conciencia popular* (Caracas, 1987); Gustavo Martín, *Magia y religión en la Venezuela contemporánea* (Caracas, 1983).
13. Marc Saint-Upéry, *El Sueño de Bolívar: El desafío de las izquierdas sudamericanas* (Barcelona, 2008) (originally published as *Le rêve de Bolívar: Le défi des gauches sud-américaines* (Paris, 2007).
14. Quoted in Hanns Heiman, "Humboldt und Bolívar: Begegnung zweier Welten in zwei Männern," in *Alexander von Humboldt. Studien zu seiner universalen Geisteshaltung*, ed. Joachim H. Schultze (Berlin, 1959), pp. 215–234, here pp. 233f.
15. Peter Blanchard, "The Slave Soldiers of Spanish South America: From Independence to Abolition," in *Arming Slaves from Classical Times to Modern Age*, ed. Christopher Brown, Leslie Christopher, and Philipp D. Morgan (New Haven, 2006), pp. 255–273.
16. James E. Sanders, "Atlantic Republicanism in Nineteenth-Century Colombia: Spanish America's Challenge to the Contours of Atlantic History," *Journal of World History* 20, no. 1 (2009): 131–150.
17. Manfred Kossok, "Alexander von Humboldt und der historische Ort der Unabhängigkeitsrevolution Lateinamerikas," in *Alexander von Humboldt: Wirkendes Vorbild für Fortschritt und Befreiung der Menschheit; Festschrift aus Anlass seines 200. Geburtstages,* edited for the Kommission für die A.-v.-Humboldt-Ehrungen 1969 der Deutschen Demokratischen Republik von der Deutschen Akademie der Wissenschaften zu Berlin (Berlin, 1969), pp. 1–26; Günter Kahle, "Simón Bolívar und Alexander von Humboldt," in *Simón Bolívar und die Deutschen* (Berlin, 1980), pp. 39–49.
18. Nicolaas A. Rupke, *Alexander von Humboldt: A Metabiography* (Frankfurt am Main, 2005).
19. Karl Marx, "Bolivar y Ponte," in Karl Marx and Friedrich Engels, *Werke*, vol. 14 (Berlin, 1972) (unchanged repr. of the 1st ed., 1961), pp. 217–231, see also http://www.mlwerke.de/me/me14/me14_217.htm (accessed March 25, 2011); José Roberto Arze, *Análisis crítico del Bolívar de Marx* (La Paz, 1998); Karl Marx, *Simón Bolívar,* introduction by José Aricó, Marcos R. Rosenmann, and Sara Martínez Cuadrado (Madrid, 2009); Max Zeuske, "Simón Bolívar und Karl Marx," in *Die Weltbühne* (Berlin, 1983), pp. 995–998; idem, "Simón Bolívar, su posición en la historia y en la actualidad," in *Interpretaciones y ensayos marxistas acerca de Simón Bolívar*, ed. Max Zeuske (Berlin, 1985) (*Asien, Afrika, Lateinamerica* special issue 14), pp. 1–20; Manfred Kossok, "Simón Bolívar, ¿el primer bonapartista de América Latina?" in Zeuske (ed.), *Interpretaciones y ensayos marx-*

istas, pp. 34–39; Manfred Kossok, "Simón Bolívar und das historische Schicksal Spanisch-Amerikas," *Ausgewählte Schriften*, ed. Matthias Middell, 3 vols. (Leipzig, 2000), pp. 251–272; Wolfgang Küttler and Matthias Middel (eds.), *Vergleichende Evolutionsgeschichte der Neuzeit*, vol. 2, pp. 251–272; Jerónimo Carrera (ed.), *Bolívar visto por marxistas* (Caracas, 1987).

20. An older but still unsurpassed synthesis of the Bolívar myth is found in the historicist book by Gerhard Masur, a German historian expelled by the Nazis: Gerhard Masur, *Simón Bolívar und die Befreiung Südamerikas* (Konstanz, 1949); see also Michael Zeuske, "Regiones, espacios e hinterland en la independencia de Venezuela: Lo espacial en la política de Simón Bolívar," *Revista de las Américas: Historia y presente*, no. 1 (2003): 39–58.
21. See also Jeremy Adelman, "Capitalism and Slavery on Imperial Hinterlands," in *Sovereignty and Revolution in the Iberian Atlantic* (Princeton, NJ, 2006), pp. 56–100.

Chapter I

1. Michael Zeuske, *Kleine Geschichte Venezuelas* (Munich, 2007); idem, *Von Bolívar zu Chávez: Die Geschichte Venezuelas* (Zürich, 2008); a very good summary of the continental processes of Independencia, including Haiti's and Brazil's, is found in Stefan Rinke, *Revolutionen in Lateinamerika: Wege in die Unabhängigkeit 1760–1860* (Munich, 2010). The book is not entirely free of a liberal-positivist view of Independencia. However, the battles of the other social and military movements came to an end neither in 1821 nor in 1825, but only in 1830.
2. Wolfgang Reinhard (ed.), *Verstaatlichung der Welt? Europäische Staatsmodelle und außereuropäische Machtprozesse* (Munich, 1999).
3. Michael Zeuske, "Conquista und Sklaverei," in *Schwarze Karibik: Sklaven, Sklavereikultur und Emanzipation* (Zürich, 2004), pp. 43–68
4. Götz Simmer, *Gold und Sklaven: Die Provinz Venezuela während der Welser-Verwaltung (1528–1556)* (Berlin, 2000); Jörg Denzer, *Die Konquista der Augsburger Welser-Gesellschaft in Südamerika 1528–1556: Historische Rekonstruktion, Historiographie und lokale Erinnerungskultur in Kolumbien und Venezuela* (Munich, 2005).
5. Michael Zeuske, "Atlantik, Sklaven und Sklaverei – Elemente einer neuen Globalgeschichte," *Jahrbuch für Geschichte der Europäischen Expansion* 6 (2006): 9–44.

6. Barbara Beuys, "Die sephardische Diaspora," in *Spanien und die Sepharden: Geschichte, Kultur, Literatur*, ed. Norbert Rehrmann and Andreas Koechert (Tübingen, 1999), pp. 51–67, here 54f.
7. Pedro Vicente Sosa Llanos, *Nos Los Inquisidores: El Santo Oficio en Venezuela* (Caracas, 2005).
8. José Oviedo y Baños, *Historia de la conquista y población de la provincia de Venezuela* (Madrid, 1723).
9. Alejandro E. Gómez, "El 'estigma africano' en los Mundos Hispano-Atlánticos (siglos XIV al XIX)," *Revista de História*, no. 153, 2º (2005): 139–180.
10. Manuel Rodríguez Campos, "Venezuela, una República en ciernes" in *La libranza del sudor: El drama de la inmigración canaria a Venezuela entre 1830 y 1859* (Santa Cruz de Tenerife, 2004), pp. 33–76.
11. Although there are many more recent, valuable investigations of Atlantic macro-trade, there still exists no deep study that deals with the subject of "original accumulation" that includes the smuggling of African slaves into the Spanish colonies. Cf. Michael Zeuske, "Out of the Americas: Sklavenhändler und Hidden Atlantic im 19. Jahrhundert. Ein Forschungsprojekt am Historischen Seminar der Universität zu Köln," http://www.ahf-muenchen.de/Forschungsberichte/Jahrbuch2009/AHF_Jb2009_Zeuske.pdf.
12. Jeremy Adelman, "Capitalism and Slavery on Imperial Hinterlands," in *Sovereignty and Revolution in the Iberian Atlantic* (Princeton, NJ, 2006), pp. 56–100; Barbara H. Stein and Stanley J. Stein, *Edge of Crisis: War and Trade in the Spanish Atlantic, 1789–1808* (Baltimore, 2009).
13. Juan Andreo García, "La capitanía General de Venezuelas y el comercio libre de negros," in *IX Congreso de Historia de América: Europa e Iberoamérica; Cinco siglos de intercambios*, ed. María J. Sarabia Viejo, 3 vols. (Seville, 1992), vol. 3, pp. 617–630.
14. Juan Ortiz and Ivana Frasquet (eds.), *Jaque a la Corona: La cuestión política en las Independencias Iberoamericanas* (Castelló de la Plana, 2010); Beatriz Bragoni, "¿Nacionalismos sin nación? Experiencias guerreras e identidades políticas en los orígenes de las naciones hispanoamericanas," in *La Corona rota: Identidades y representaciones en las Independencias Iberoamericanas*, ed. Marta Terán and Victor Gayol (Castelló de la Plana, 2010), pp. 21–40.
15. David B. Gaspar and David P. Geggus, *A Turbulent Time: The French Revolution and the Greater Caribbean* (Bloomington, IN, 1996); David P. Geggus (ed.), *The Impact of the Haitian Revolution in the Atlantic World* (Colombia, 2001); Alejandro E. Gómez, "La Revolu-

ción Haitiana y la Tierra Firme hispana," *Nuevo Mundo Mundos Nuevos*, no. 5 (2005), http://nuevomundo.revues.org/document211. html (accessed June 29, 2006); idem, "Haïti: entre la peur et le besoin; Royalistes et républicains vénézuéliens: relations et repères avec Saint-Domingue et les 'Îles du Vent', 1790–1830," in *La Révolution haïtienne au-delà de ses frontières*, ed. Giulia Bonacci (Paris, 2006), pp. 141–163.
16. Alejandro E. Gómez, "Las revoluciones blanqueadoras: elites mulatas haitianas y 'pardos beneméritos' venezolanos, y su aspiración a la igualdad, 1789–1812," in *Nuevo Mundo Mundos Nuevos, Coloquios* (2005), http://www.nuevomundo.revues.org/index868.html (accessed September 23, 2009); idem, "The 'Pardo question,' " in *Nuevo Mundo Mundos Nuevos, Materiales de seminarios* (2008), http://www.nuevomundo.revues.org/index34503.html (accessed September 23, 2009); Clément Thibaud, " 'Coupé têtes, brûlé cazes': Peurs et désirs d'Haïti dans l'Amérique de Bolívar," *Annales: Histoire, Sciences sociales* 58, no. 2 (2003): 305–331.
17. Frédérique Langue, "Humboldt und der 'Afrikanerstaat' Venezuela: bürgerliche Zwiste und feindselige Leidenschaften," *Comparativ: Leipziger Beiträge zur Universalgeschichte und zur vergleichenden Gesellschaftsforschung* 11, fasc. 2 (2001): pp. 16–29.
18. Michael Zeuske, "Vater der Unabhängigkeit? Humboldt und die Transformation zur Moderne im spanischen Amerika," in *Alexander von Humboldt: Aufbruch in die Moderne*, ed. Ottmar Ette, Ute Hermanns, Bernd Scherer, and Christian Suckow (Berlin, 2001), pp. 179–224.
19. Margot Faak (ed.), *Alexander von Humboldt, Reise durch Venezuela: Auswahl aus den amerikanischen Reisetagebüchern* (Berlin, 2000).
20. Michael Zeuske, "Vergleichen oder Vernetzen? Der Vergleich der Sklavereien in den Amerikas in historischer Perspektive," *Zeitschrift für Weltgeschichte: Interdisziplinäre Perspektiven* 7, no. 1 (2006): 15–56.
21. Idem: "¿Humboldtcanización del mundo occidental? La importancia del viaje de Humboldt para Europa y América Latina," in *Francisco de Miranda y la modernidad en América: introducción, selección, transcripción y notas* (Madrid, 2004), pp. 13–106; idem, "Humboldt, esclavitud, autonomismo y emancipación en las Américas, 1791–1825," in *Alexander von Humboldt: Estancia en España y viaje americano*, ed. Mariano Cuesta Domingo and Sandra Rebok (Madrid, 2008), pp. 257–277.
22. Frédérique Langue, *Las élites de Venezuela y la revolución francesa o la formación de un ideal democrático* (Caracas, 1990); idem, "Les

identités fractales: Honneur et couleur dans la société vénézuélienne du XVIIIe siècle," *Caravelle* 65 (1995), pp. 23–37.
23. On Humboldt's interculturalism, see Ottmar Ette, *Weltbewußtsein: Alexander von Humboldt und das unvollendete Projekt einer anderen Moderne* (Weilerswist, 2002); on Humboldt's unclear boundaries, see Oliver Lubrich, "Dolores, enfermedades y metáforas poéticas del cuerpo en Alejandro de Humboldt," *Revista de Indias* 64, no. 231 (2004): 503–528.
24. Christian Geulen, *Wahlverwandte: Rassendiskurs und Nationalismus im späten 19. Jahrhundert* (Hamburg, 2004).
25. Michael Zeuske, "Comparando el Caribe: Alexander von Humboldt, Saint-Domingue y los comienzos de la comparación de la esclavitud en las Américas," *Estudos Afro-Asiáticos* 26, no. 2 (2004): 381–416; idem, "Alexander von Humboldt y la comparación de las esclavitudes en las Américas," *Humboldt im Netz* 6, no. 11 (2005): 65–89, http://www.unipotsdam.de/u/romanistik/humboldt/hin/hin11/inh_zeuske.htm; idem, "Humboldt, esclavitud, autonomismo y emancipación en las Américas, 1791–1825," in *Alexander von Humboldt: Estancia en España y viaje americano*, ed. Mariano Cuesta Domingo and Sandra Rebok (Madrid, 2008), pp. 257–277; idem, "Comparing or Interlinking? Economic Comparisons of Early Nineteenth-Century Slave Systems in the Americas in Historical Perspective," in *Slave Systems: Ancient and Modern*, Enrico Dal Lago and Constantina Katsari (Cambridge, 2008), pp. 148–183.
26. Idem, "Arango y Humboldt/Humboldt y Arango: Ensayos científicos sobre la esclavitud." in *Francisco de Arango y la invención de la Cuba azucarera*, ed. María Dolores González-Ripoll and Izaskun Álvarez Cuartero (Salamanca, 2009), pp. 245–260; see also Sandra Rebok, "La Révolution de Haïti vue par deux personnages contemporains: Le scientifique prussien Alexander von Humboldt et l'homme d'état américain Thomas Jefferson," in *French Colonial History* 10 (2009): 75–95.
27. The leader of the expedition, who died of yellow fever.
28. "Todos mueren, y así sucedía desde los últimos tiempos del General Leclerc: lo más dulce para estos infelices es ser pasado por las armas, y todavía no es lo peor que espalda con espalda, y de dos en dos, sean arrojados al mar. Lo que me estremece es haber oído de la boca del Jefe de Brigada Nerau, Comandante de la Guardia del General en Jefe, que la noche antes había echado a los perros una negra prisionera; y otra ... que en aquella mañana había sorprendido un destacamento de doce insurgentes, cuyo Jefe fue entregado a la tropa que lo pidió para sacarle, vivo, los ojos." Francisco de Arango y Parreño:

"Comisión de Arango en Santo Domingo," in *Obras de D. Francisco de Arango y Parreño*, 2 vols. (Havana, 1952), vol. 1, pp. 344–383, here p. 363; see also José Antonio Piqueras Arenas, "La misión de Guarico y el nacimiento del buen esclavista cubano," *Ibero-Americana Pragensia*, supp. 25 (2009): 139–156.

29. Original in French: "Le Terrorisme regnait en 1803 aux Colonies." Cf. "Isle de Cube. Antilles en géneral" (Humboldt, Alexander, Tagebuch 1804), in Biblioteka Jagiellonska Kraków, oddzial Rekopisów, 1161, Al. v. Humboldt Nachlaß 3, f. 15r.
30. Mario Briceño Iragorry, *La tragedia de Peñalver* (Bogotá, 1949); Alarico Gómez, *Fernando Penalver, 1761–1837* (Caracas, 1973).
31. Peñalver was a merchant.
32. Humboldt refers to the reintroduction of slavery into France and its colonies, which actually took place in 1802, at Napoleon's command; see Gustav Roloff, *Die Kolonialpolitik Napoleons I* (Munich, 1899), pp. 244–254; appendix, "Napoleon's secret instructions to Geneeral Leclerc, 9 Brumaire, year 10 (31 October 1801)."
33. Alexander von Humboldt, "Von Caracas an den See von Valencia und nach Puerto Cabello (7.2.–5.3.1800)," *Reise durch Venezuela: Auswahl aus den amerikanischen Reisetagebüchern*, ed. Margot Faak (Berlin, 2000), pp. 185–221, here p. 208.
34. "G[enera]l B[olívar]. – esteemed Peñalver as one of his best friends and the best of men. It was P[eñalver] – who advised him to convoke a congress in 1819. P[eñalver] – was one of the few who thoued (*tuteaba*) Gl B[olívar]-." Cf. Robert Arthur Humphreys (ed.), *The "Detached Recollections" of General D. F. O'Leary* (London, 1969), p. 29.
35. Lucas G. Castillo Lara, "El Negro Miguel Guacamaya y su Cumbe," in *Apuntes para la historia colonial de Barlovento* (Caracas, 1981), pp. 619–621; Angel Sanz Tapia, "Refugiados de la Revolución Francesa en Venezuela (1793–1795)," *Revista de Indias* 47, no. 3 (1987), pp. 833–868.
36. "El Gobernador [de la Habana], Conde de Santa Clara: Da cuenta del apresamiento de una Goleta Correo, q.e de la Guayra salió p.a Pto. Rico, por una Fragata Ynglesa, Havana 1º de Febrero de 1797," Archivo General de Indias (AGI), Sevilla, Estado, p. 1 (1729–1860), Estado 1: Santo Domingo, Cuba, Puerto Rico, Luisiana y Florida: "Documentación de la 1ª Secretaría de Estado relativa al ámbito geográfico de Santo Domingo, Cuba, Puerto Rico, Luisiana y Florida. Contiene la correspondencia cruzada entre el Secretario de Estado y las autoridades de estas provincias de América, en las que se dá cuenta de los primeros movimientos independentistas," 1, n. 5.

37. Report by the businessman Heinrich Rötgers from San Tomás regarding the Miranda Expedition, Dahlem, Geheimes Staatsarchiv (GStA), Rep. XI, 21b, 5, Central America (1806) (without foliation).
38. Archivo General de Simancas, Spanien (AGS), Secretaría Guerra, p. 114 (1771–1804), Venezuela: "Fechos, empleos y retiros; correspondencia con los capitanes generales y gobernadores; arreglo de milicias; emigrados Franceses de Martinica y prisioneros de Santo Domingo; gobierno y sublevación de Coro."
39. Keith O. Laurence, "Colonialism in Trinidad and Tobago," *Caribbean Quarterly* 9, no. 3 (1963): 44–56; Bridget Brereton, *A History of Modern Trinidad, 1783–1962* (Port of Spain, 1981); María D. González-Ripoll Navarro, *Trinidad: La otra llave de América* (Caracas, 1992); John A. Meredith, *The Plantation Slaves of Trinidad, 1783 to 1816* (New York, 1988); Keith O. Laurence, *Tobago in Wartime, 1793 to 1815* (Kingston, 1995).
40. "Aranj.z 28 de Mayo de 1791, del Govern.or Cap.n Gener.l de Guyana," Archivo General de Indias, Estado, 63 (06/1750–26.01.1830), Estado, Caracas: "Documentos de la Secretaría de Estado relativos a la Audiencia de Caracas (Alborotos contra la Compañía de Caracas. Sublevaciones en las provincias de Caracas. Miranda y el levantamiento de Caracas. Memorial de Francisco de Azpurua sobre los medios de recuperar las Américas. Separación de Venezuela del gobierno de Bogotá)," N. 2,2.
41. Federico Brito Figueroa, "Las rebeliones de esclavos en Venezuela colonial," in *El problema tierra y esclavos en la historia de Venezuela* (Caracas, 1985), pp. 205–250; Gerardo Acuña, *La esclavitud: El negro Guillermo de Barlovento* (Caracas, 1993).
42. Michael Zeuske, "Francisco de Miranda (1750–1816): América, Europa und die Globalisierung der ersten Entkolonialisierung," in *Globale Lebensläufe: Menschen als Akteure im weltgeschichtlichen Geschehen*, ed. Bernd Hausberger (Vienna, 2006), pp. 117–142.
43. Inés Quintero, "Representación y ciudadanía: Venezuela 1808–1814," in *Jaque a la Corona:. La cuestión política en las independencias Iberoamericanas*, ed. Juan Ortiz and Ivana Frasquet (Castellón 2010), pp. 103–122; Diana Carolyn Cifuentes López, "Real Audiencia de Santa fé durante las revoluciones hispánicas (1808–1819)," in ibid., pp. 123–149; Ligia Berbesí de Salazar, "Representación política, conflictos y opinión en la construcción de la república Venezuela, 1808–1812," in *La corona rota: Identidades y representaciones en las independecias Iberoamericana*s, ed. Marta Terán and Víctor Gayol (Castellón, 2010), pp. 109–131.
44. Arlene Q. Urdaneta and German Cardozo Galué, "El federalismo du-

rante la indepencia de Venezuela: Rivalidades regionales y negociación política," in *Colectivos sociales y participación popular en la independencia hispanoamericana*, ed. Arlene Q. Urdaneta and German Cardozo Galué (Maracaibo, 2005), pp. 127–146.
45. Alejandro E. Gómez, "La Revolución de Caracas desde abajo," *Nuevo Mundo Mundos Nuevos,* Debates (2008), http://www.nuevomundo.revues.org/index32982.html (accessed September 23, 2009).
46. José F. Heredia, *Memorias del Regente Heredia* (Caracas, 1986); "Acta de Independencia [1811]," in Germán Carrera Damas, *De la Abolición de la Monarquía hacia la instauración de la República 1810–1830* (Caracas, 2009), pp. 43–53, here p. 44.
47. François-Xavier Guerra, "El escrito de la revolución y la revolución del escrito: Información, propaganda y opinión pública en el mundo hispánico (1808–1914)," in *Las guerras de indepedencia en la América Española*, ed. Marta Terán and José Antonio Serrano Ortega (Zamora, 2001), pp. 125–147; François-Xavier Guerra, "La ruptura originaria: Mutaciones, debates y mitos de la Independencia," in *Visiones y revisiones de la Independencia Americana*, ed. Izaskun Álvarez Cuartero and Julio Sánchez Gómez (Salamanca, 2003), pp. 89–110.
48. José A. Piqueras, *Bicentenarios de Libertad: La fragua de la política en España y las Américas* (Barcelona, 2010).
49. Arlene J. Díaz, "Vicenta ochoa, Dead Many Times: Gender, Politics, and Death Sentence in Early Republican Caracas, Venezuela," in *Gender, Sexuality, and Power in Latin America since Independence*, ed. William E. French and Katherine Elaine Bliss (Lanham, MD, 2007), pp. 31–51.
50. Germán Carrera Damas, *De la Abolición de la Monarquía hacia la instauración de la República 1810–1830* (Caracas, 2009), pp. 43–53.
51. Julio Febres Cordero, *El primer ejército republicano y la campaña de Coro* (Caracas, 1973); Ines Quintero, "La primera derrota del marqués," in *El último marqués: Francisco Rodríguez del Toro (1761–1851)* (Caracas, 2005), pp. 112–116.
52. John V. Lombardi, "Los esclavos negros en las guerras venezolanas de la Independencia," *Cultura Universitaria* 93 (1966), pp. 153–168.
53. Pablo Rodríguez, "1812: el terremoto que interrumpió una revolución," *Una historia de los usos del miedo*, ed. Pilar Gonzalbo Aizpuru, Anne Staples, and Valentina Torres Septién (México, 2009), pp. 247–271.
54. The most important eyewitness testimony to this time—which has hardly been noticed and which, moreover, forgoes myth building around Bolívar—is found in the book by the German-Danish physi-

cian Friedrich Mayer, who was the first to perform an autopsy in Caracas. Cf. also Henri Poudenx and Friedrich Mayer, *Mémoires pour servir à l'histoire de la révolution de la Capitanerie Générale de Caracas, depuis l'abdication de Charles IV jusqu'au mois d'aout 1814* (Paris, 1815).

55. William F. Lewis, "Simón Bolívar and Xavier Mina. A Rendezvous in Haiti," *Journal of Inter-American Studies and World Affairs* 11, no. 3 (1969): 458–465.
56. Tulio Arends, *La República de las Floridas (1817–1818)* (Caracas, 1986).
57. Teresa Sonta-Jaroszewicz, "Militares polacos al servicio de Miranda y Bolívar en la guerra de Independencia," *Tiempos de América: Revista de Historia, Cultura y Territorio*, no. 16 (2009): 25–38.
58. Ursula Acosta, "Ducoudray Holstein: Hombre al margen de la historia." *Revista de Historia* (San Juan, Puerto Rico) 1, no. 2 (1985): 63–89; Guillermo A. Baralt, "Ducoudray Holstein y la Noche de San Miguel," in *Esclavos rebeldes: Conspiraciones y sublevaciones de esclavos en Puerto Rico (1795–1873)* (Río Piedras, 1985), pp. 47ff. Born Pierre Villaume, the son of a Huguenot pastor in Brandenburg or Schwedt, he died in France—an enigmatic person.
59. Henry L. V. Ducoudray Holstein, *Bolívar's Denkwürdigkeiten: die Charakterschilderung und Thaten des Süd-Amerikanischen Helden, die geheime Geschichte der Revolution in Colombia und ein Sittengemälde des Colombischen Volkes enthaltend*, 2 vols. (Hamburg, 1830).
60. Karl Marx, "Bolivar y Ponte," in Karl Marx and Friedrich Engels, *Werke*, vol. 14 (Berlin, 1972) (repr. of the 1961 original), pp. 217–231.
61. Paul Verna, *Monsieur Bideau, el mulato francés que fue el segundo organizador de la Expedición de Chacachacare* (Caracas, 1968); idem, *Tres franceses en la historia de Venezuela* (Caracas, 1973).
62. Jesús C. Torres Almeyda, *El almirante José Padilla: epopeya y martirio* (Bogotá, 1983).
63. Mark Häberlein and Michaela Schmölz-Häberlein, "Zwischen zwei Kriegen," in *Die Erben der Welser: Der Karibikhandel der Augsburger Firma Obwexer im Zeitalter der Revolutionen* (Augsburg, 1995), pp. 83–100; Manuel Díaz Ugueto, *Luis Brión, almirante de la libertad* (Caracas, 1993).
64. Jane Lucas de Grummond, *Renato Beluche: Smuggler; privateer and patriot* (Baton Rouge, LA, 1983).
65. Eric Lambert, *Voluntarios británicos e irlandeses en la gesta Bolivariana* (Caracas, 1981).

66. Feliciano Gámez Duarte, "Corsarios en las guerras de independencia de Hispanoamérica: Entre el patriotismo y la delincuencia," in *La Ilusión Constitucional: Pueblo, Patria, Nación; De la Ilustración al Romanticismo, Cádiz, América y Europa ante la modernidad, 1750–1850* (Cádiz, 2004), pp. 251–262.
67. Paul Verna, *Bolívar y los emigrados patriotas en el Caribe (Trinidad, Curazao, San Thomas, Jamaica, Haití)* (Caracas, 1983).
68. The movement and the role of the republican pardos and mulattos have been most thoroughly investigated for modern Colombia, especially for Cartagena and the Caribbean coast. See Alfonso Múnera, *El fracaso de la nación: Región, clase y raza en el Caribe colombiano (1717 a 1810)* (Santa Fe de Bogotá, 1998); idem, "José Ignacio de Pombo y Francisco José de Caldas: Pobladores de las tinieblas," in *Fronteras imaginadas: La construcción de las razas y de la geografía en el siglo XIX colombiano* (Bogotá, 2005), pp. 45–88; Marixa Lasso, "Haiti as an Image of Popular Republicanism in Caribbean Colombia: Cartagena Province (1811–1828)," in David P. Geggus, *The Impact of the Haitian Revolution in the Atlantic World* (Columbia, SC, 2001), pp. 176–190; Marixa Lasso, *Myths of Harmony: Race and Republicanism during the Age of Revolution, Colombia 1795–1831* (Pittsburgh, 2007); for Venezuela, see Alejandro E. Gómez, "La Revolución de Caracas desde abajo," *Nuevo Mundo Mundos Nuevos*, Debates (2008), http://nuevomundo.revues.org/32982 (accessed September 23, 2009).
69. However, the slave rebellions have been very little studied from the point of view of the slaves. Cf. Peter Blanchard, "The Slave Soldiers of Spanish South America: From Independence to Abolition," in *Arming Slaves from Classical Times to Modern Age*, ed. Christopher L. Brown and Philip D. Morgan (New Haven, CT, 2006), pp. 255–273; idem, "Serving the King in Venezuela and New Granada," in *Under the Flags of Freedom: Slave Soldiers in Wars of Independence in Spanish South America* (Pittsburgh, 2008), pp. 17–36.
70. Miguel Izard, *Orejanos, cimarrones y arrochelados* (Barcelona, 1988).
71. Tomás Pérez Tenreiro, *Para acercarnos a don Francisco Tomás Morales mariscal de campo, último capitán general en la tierra firme y a José Tomás Boves coronel, primera lanza del Rey* (Caracas, 1994).
72. Caracciolo Parra-Pérez, *Historia de la Primera República de Venezuela*, with Cristóbal L. Mendoza and Rafael Ángel Rivas (Caracas, 1992), p. 499.
73. José Ambrosio Llamozas, "Memorial presentado al rey en Madrid,"

Boletín de la Academia Nacional de La Historia (BANH) (Caracas) 5 (1921): 515–529; idem, "Memorial presentado al rey en Madrid por Pbro. Doctor Don José Ambrosio Llamozas, vicario general del ejército de Varlovento, en las provincias de Venezuela [1815]," in *Antología Documental de Venezuela 1492–1900: Materiales para la enseñanza de la historia de Venezuela*, ed. Santos R. Cortés (Caracas, 1960), pp. 220–230; José Mercedes Gómez, *La guerra de independencia en el Oriente: El conflicto entre los libertadores* (Cumaná, 1991).

74. José A. de Armas Chitty, "El tremendo Memorial," in *Historia del Guarico*, 2 vols. (San Juan de los Morros, 1978), vol. 2, pp. 19–22.
75. Federico Brito Figueroa, "La contribución de Laureano Vallenilla Lanz a la comprensión histórica de Venezuela," in Laureano Vallenilla Lanz, *Obras Completas*, 3 vols. (Caracas, 1983–1988), vol. 1, pp. iii–xxiv, here p. xvii.
76. James E. Sanders, "Atlantic Republicanism in Nineteenth-Century Colombia: Spanish America's Challenge to the Contours of Atlantic History," *Journal of World History* 20, no. 1 (2009): 131–150.
77. Gonzalo Quintero Saravia, *Pablo Morillo: General de dos mundos* (Bogotá, 2005).
78. Michael Riekenberg, *Caudillismus: Eine kurze Abhandlung anhand des La Plata-Raumes* (Leipzig, 2010).
79. Michael Riekenberg, "Kriegerische Gewaltakteure in Lateinamerika im frühen 19. Jahrhundert," in *Kulturen der Gewalt. Ritualisierung und Symbolisierung von Gewalt in der Geschichte*, ed. Rolf P. Sieferle and Helga Breuninger (Frankfurt am Main, 1998), pp. 195–214.
80. Mariano Picón Salas, *Los días de Cipriano Castro (Historia venezolana del 1900)* (Caracas, 1953), p. 148.
81. Edgar Esteves González, *Las guerras de los caudillos* (Caracas, 2006).
82. Simón Bolívar, " 'Decreto de Guerra a Muerte', Trujillo, 15. Juni 1813," in *Decretos del Libertador*, ed. Comité Regional Bicentenario del Natalicio del Libertador (Estado Miranda), 3 vols. (Los Teques, 1983), vol. 1, pp. 5–9.
83. "Españoles y Canarios, contad con la muerte, aún siendo indiferentes, si no obrais activamente en obsequio de la libertad de Venezuela. Americanos, contad con la vida, aún cuando seais culpables," ibid., p. 9.
84. Véronique Hébrard, *Le Venezuela independent: Une nation par le discours, 1808–1830*, pref. by F.-X. Guerra (Paris, 1996); Clemént Thibaud, "De la ficción al mito: los llaneros de la Independencia en Venezuela," *Tiempos de América* 10 (2003): 109–119.

85. Catalina Banko, "Alderson, John," in *Diccionario de Historia de Venezuela*, ed. Manuel Rodríguez Campos, 4 vols. (Caracas, 1997), vol. 1, p. 107; see also the memoir by Thomas R. Ybarra, *Young Man of Caracas* (Camden, 1941).
86. Michael Zeuske, "Simón Bolívar in Geschichte, Mythos und Kult," in *Vielstimmige Vergangenheiten: Geschichtspolitik in Lateinamerika*, ed. Berthold Molden and David Mayer, vol. 12 of *¡Atención! Jahrbuch des Österreichischen Lateinamerika-Instituts* (Münster, 2009), pp. 241–265; Arlene Díaz, "Vicenta Ochoa, Dead Many Times: Gender, Politics, and Death Sentence in Early Republican Caracas, Venezuela," in *Gender, Sexuality, and Power in Latin America, 1760–Present*, ed. Katherine Bliss and William Französisch (Lanham, 2006), pp. 31–51.
87. Martha Abreu, "Slave Mothers and Freed Children: Emancipation and Female Space in Debates on the 'Free Womb' Law, Rio de Janeiro, 1871," *Journal of Latin American Studies* 28 (1996): 567–580.
88. Michael Zeuske, "Eliten, Sklaverei und Land," in *Von Bolívar zu Chávez: Die Geschichte Venezuelas* (Zürich, 2008), pp. 167–183; on the debates regarding slavery at congresses and in laws, see José Marcial Ramos Guédez, "Simón Bolívar: La abolición de la esclavitud en Venezuela 1810–1830; Problemas y frustración de una causa," *Revista de Historia de América* 125 (Jul.–Dec. 1999): 7–20; Pedro Felipe Hoyos Körbel, "Bolívar y la legislación esclavista," in *Bolívar y las negritudes: Momentos históricos de una minoria étnica en la Gran Colombia* (Manizales, 2007), pp. 228–330.
89. Aline Helg, "Simón Bolívar and the Spectre of Pardocracia: José Padilla in Post-Independenca Cartagena," *Journal of Latin American Studies* 35, no. 3 (2003): 447–471.
90. Alexander von Humboldt, *Reise in die Äquinoktial-Gegenden des Neuen Kontinents*, ed. O. Ette, 2 vols. (Frankfurt am Main, 1999).
91. Michael Zeuske, "Vater der Unabhängigkeit? Humboldt und die Transformation zur Moderne im spanischen Amerika," in *Alexander von Humboldt: Aufbruch in die Moderne*, ed. Ottmar Ette, Ute Hermanns, Bernd Scherer, and Christian Suckow (Berlin, 2001), pp. 179–224.
92. Federico Brito Figueroa, *Tiempo de Ezequiel Zamora* (Caracas, 1981).
93. Tomás Straka, " 'La Francia del Sur': Civilización, occidentalidad y Proyecto Nacional de Venezuela (1870–1899)," in *La Historia y el despliegue occidental: Cultura, narrativa y eseñanza*, ed. Jorge Bracho (Caracas, 2009), pp. 121–150.

94. Michael Zeuske, "Ein aufgeklärter Autokrat und die Entstehung des modernen Venezuela (1870–1908)," in *Von Bolívar zu Chávez: Die Geschichte Venezuelas* (Zürich, 2008), pp. 283–328.
95. Tomás Straka, " 'La Francia del Sur': Civilización, occidentalidad y Proyecto Nacional de Venezuela (1870–1899)," in *La Historia y el despliegue occidental: Cultura, narrativa y eseñanza*, ed. Jorge Bracho (Caracas, 2009), pp. 121–150.
96. Rafael A. Rondón Marquéz, *La esclavitud en Venezuela, el proceso de su abolición y las personalidades de sus decisivos propulsores: José Gregorio Monagas y Simón Planas* (Caracas, 1954); Miguel A. Ortega, *La esclavitud en el contexto agropecuario colonial: siglo XVIII* (Caracas, 1992); José Ramos Guédez, *El negro en Venezuela: aporte bibliográfico* (Caracas, 1985); idem, *José Silverio González y la abolición de la esclavitud en Venezuela, 1850–1854* (Caracas, 1990); B. U. Torrealba Rosales, *Aproximación al estudio de la ley de manumisión como instrumento de la oligarquía: Turmero 1830–1848* (Maracay, 1988); Michael Zeuske, "Die *Herrschaft der Monagas-Brüder (1848–1858)*," in *Von Bolívar zu Chávez: Die Geschichte Venezuelas* (Zürich, 2008), pp. 225–242.
97. See the pictures of Bolívar reproduced in the Bolívar archive of Daniel Florencio O'Leary, *Memorias del General O'Leary, publicadas por su hijo Simón B. O'Leary, por orden del gobierno de Venezuela y bajo los auspicios de su presidente General Guzmán Blanco, Ilustre Americano, Regenerador de la República*, 32 vols. (Caracas, 1882; repr. as *Memorias del General O'Leary, edición facsimilar del original de la primera edición, con motivo de la celebración del Sesquicentenario de la Muerte de Simón Bolívar, Padre de la Patria*, 34 vols., Caracas 1981).
98. Laureano Vallenilla Lanz, "El gendarme necesario," in *Obras Completas*, vol. 1, pp. 79–94; Federico Brito Figueroa, "La contribución de Laureano Vallenilla Lanz a la comprensión histórica de Venezuela," in ibid., vol. 1, pp. iii–xxiv; Laureano Vallenilla Lanz, "Cesarismo democático. Estudios sobre las bases sociológicas de la constitución efectiva de Venezuela," in *Cesarismo democrático y otros textos: Prólogo, notas, cronología y bibliografía*, Biblioteca Ayacucho, vol. 164 (Caracas, 1991), pp. 9–149; on the influence of this concept, see Luciano Canfora, *Caesar: Der demokratische Diktator; Eine Biografie* (Munich, 2001).
99. Antonio J. Torrealba Osto, *Diario de un Llanero*, ed. E. Colmenares del Valle, 6 vols. (Caracas, 1987).
100. Naudy Suárez Figueroa, *La Generación del 28 y otras generaciones: Antología de textos* (Caracas, 2008).

101. Fernando Coronil, *The Magic State: Nature, Money, and Modernity in Venezuela* (Chicago, 1997).
102. Karl Marx and Friedrich Engels, *Werke* (Berlin, 1961), vol. 14, pp. 217–231; Karl Marx, *Simón Bolívar*, introd. by J. Aricó, R. Rosenmann, and S. Martínez Cuadrado (Madrid, 2009); Max Zeuske, "Simón Bolívar and Karl Marx," in *Die Weltbühne* (Berlin, 1983), pp. 995–998; Manfred Kossok, "Simón Bolívar und das historische Schicksal Spanisch-Amerikas," *Ausgewählte Schriften*, ed. Matthias Middell, vol. 2 (Leipzig, 2000), pp. 251–272; Inés Quintero, "Bolívar de izquierda, Bolívar de derecha: Nación y construcción discursiva," http://www.Simón-Bolívar.org/Principal/Bolívar/bolizbolder.html (accessed September 19, 2009); idem, *El Bolívar de Marx: Estudios críticos de Inés Quintero y Vladimir Acosta* (Caracas, 2007); Tomás Straka, *La épica del desencanto* (Caracas, 2009); Michael Zeuske, "Simón Bolívar in Geschichte, Mythos und Kult," in Molden and Mayer (eds.), *Vielstimmige Vergangenheiten?* pp. 241–265.

Chapter II

1. Juan Morales Álvarez, "Los testamentos coloniales venezolanos," in *La religiosidad de los siglos XVIII y XIX: En el marco del Bicentenario de la independencia*, ed. Laura Febres (Caracas, 2009), pp. 323–338.
2. For ten years (1765–1775), Juan Vicente Bolívar was a kind of customs officer (*contador de la Real Hacienda de Caracas*) in La Guaira. All customs officers got rich through corruption and bribery; Juan Vicente declared 258,000 pesos in his will (by modern standards, that made him a millionaire several times over). In addition, he owned enormous amounts of land. See Gerardo Vivas Pineda, "Los negocios de Juan Vicente Bolívar y Ponte," *Desafío de la Historia* 2, no. 11 (2009): 28–34; idem, *La aventura naval de la Compañía Guipuzcoana de Caracas* (Caracas, 1998); as well as excerpts from the official documents under "Coronel Juan Vicente de Bolívar y Ponte," http://www.sologenealogia.com (accessed February 15, 2011).
3. Ana C. Ojeda Avellaneda, "Raíces Culturales e Históricas de la Formación del Mito," in idem, *El mito Bolivariano en la literatura latinoamericana: Aproximaciones* (Bucaramanga, 2002), pp. 36–68.
4. Juan Morales, "La mala amistad con varias mujeres solteras y casadas de todas las castas y colores de Don Juan Vicente Bolívar," *Anuario de Estudios Bolivarianos*: *Bolivarium Año VIII*, no. 9 (2000): 205–214.

5. Ibid., p. 210.
6. Inés Quintero, "Huérfana y acaudelada," in *La criolla principal: María Antonia Bolívar, Hermana del Libertador* (Caracas, 2003), pp. 18ff.
7. "El deseo de gloria es en Bolívar una idea fija, una inclinación constante de su personalidad, el vector eterno de sus actos históricos." Cf. Germán Carrera Damas, *El culto a Bolívar* (Caracas, 2003), p. 87.
8. Rafael Urdaneta, *Los Amores de Simón Bolívar* (Caracas, 1987).
9. Contemporaries and Bolívar himself wrote "Bolivar" (without the accent on the "i").
10. Rafael Urdaneta, "Llegó Simóncito, tan guapo," in *Los Amores*, pp. 253–264.
11. Jörg Denzer, "Die Zeugnisse: Genetisches Erbe der deutschen Konquistadoren?" in *Die Konquista der Augsburger Welser-Gesellschaft in Südamerika 1528–1556: Historische Rekonstruktion, Historiographie und Lokale Erinnerungskultur in Kolumbien und Venezuela*, Schriftenreihe zur Zeitschrift für Unternehmensgeschichte, vol. 15 (Munich, 2005), p. 308; also idem, "Die Diskussion um die 'deutschen Gene,'" in ibid, pp. 309ff.; Michael Zeuske, "Los Bélzares: De la colonización al saqueo de la realidad al mito," in *El Dorado: Sueños y realidades*, ed. Ulrich Gmünder (Caracas, 2007), pp. 44–51.
12. In German historiography, I mention for instance the publications of Eberhard Schmitt, Götz Simmer, Mark Häberlein, Johannes Burghardt, and Jörg Denzer, who are continuing a tradition that exists since Häbler; see Konrad Häbler, *Die Überseeischen Unternehmungen des Welser und ihrer Gesellschafter* (Leipzig, 1903).
13. Rafael L. Fuentes Carvallo, *La estirpe manchega y la sangre alemana del Libertador* (Caracas, 1976).
14. Orlando Marín Castañeda, "La casa de la familia Blanco en la Plazuela de San Jacinto de Caracas: La consolidación de una morada mantuana durante la colonia (1610–1713)," *Anuario de Estudios Bolívarianos: Bolívarium Año VIII*, no. 9 (2000): 169–203.
15. Gerhard Masur, "Youth," in *Simón Bolívar* (Albuquerque, NM, 1948), pp. 28–45, here p. 29.
16. Ana C. Ojeda Avellaneda, "Origen del hombre convertido en héroe," in *El mito Bolívariano en la literatura latinoamericana: Aproximaciones* (Bucaramanga, 2002), pp. 19–36, here pp. 25–33.
17. Manuel R. Rivero, *Matea* (Caracas, 1975); idem, *Hilachas de historia patria* (Caracas, 1983); Carlos Gómez Botero, *La infancia del Libertador y la Negra Hipólita* (Medellín, 1988).

18. "Testamento del Canónigo Don Juan Félix Jérez de Aristeguieta," in *Papeles de Bolívar*, ed. Vincente Lecuna, 2 vols. (Madrid, 1920), vol. 2, pp. 194–201; Juan Morales Álvarez, "Los bienes del mayorazgo de la Concepción," http://www.bicentenariodelasamericas. org/index.php?option=com_content&view=article&id=425:kl&catid =288:Bolívar&Itemid=329 (accessed December 13, 2010).
19. Elizabeth Ladera de Diez, *Contribución al estudio de la aristocracia territorial en la Venezuela colonial: La familia Xeréz de Aristiguieta, siglo XVIII* (Caracas, 1990).
20. Juan Morales Álvarez, "La Primera Propiedad de Simón Bolívar: El Mayorazgo de la Concepción," *Revista de Control Fiscal: Órgano de la Contraloría General de la República* 24, no. 110 (1983): 135–149; idem, *El Mayarazgo del padre Aristeguieta primera herencia del Libertador* (Caracas, 1999).
21. "Apéndice Documental: Cuadernos de inventarios referente a los bienes libres y vinculados pertenecientes al menor don Simón Bolívar," *Revista de Control Fiscal: Órgano de la Contraloría General de la República* 24, no. 110 (1983): 151–184.
22. "Yo pertenezco ahora a la familia de Colombia y no a la familia Bolívar; ya no soy de Caracas sola, soy de toda la nación," letter written from Cuenca to Fernando Toro, September 23, 1822, in Simón Bolívar, *Obras Completas*, 3 vols. (Caracas, 1982), vol. 1, pp. 683ff.
23. Richard Rosa, "A seis grados de Andrés Bello: Literatura y finanzas en los 1820," in *Nación y Literatura: Itinerarios de la palabra escrita en la cultura venezolana*, ed. Carlos Pacheco, Luis Barrera Linares, and Beatriz González Stephan (Caracas, 2006), pp. 133–152.
24. On the night of July 30, 1812, Miranda was arrested and gave Bolívar full authority to decide what was to be done with his property. The document shows him to still be fully a slave owner: "Instrucciones ...," in *Escritos del Libertador*, vol. 2, pp. 211–214.
25. Inés Quintero, "María Antonia Bolívar, la hermana del Libertador: Una 'Heroina de la Lealtad,' " *Tiempos de América: Revista de Historia, Cultura y Territorio*, no. 17 (2010): 95–103.
26. José M. Ramos Guédez, "Simón Bolívar y la abolición de la esclavitud en Venezuela 1810–1830: Problemas y frustración de una causa," *Revista de Historia de América* 125 (1999): 7–20.
27. For example, in the special power of attorney that Bolívar granted his nephew Anacleto Clemente on July 5, 1821; "Poder especial conferido a su sobrino el capitán Anacleto Clemente," Caracas, 5 de julio de 1821 (Doc. 93), in *Escritos del Libertador*, vol. 2, pp. 247f.
28. In addition, there are two eyewitness testimonies to the emancipation of 1821, ratified in 1827: "Testimonio de concesión de libertad a

María Jacinta Bolívar, esclava, librado en Caracas, en ratificación del que habia dado seis años antes," ibid., vol. 3, p. 143; "Testimonio de concesión de libertad a Francisca Barbara Bolívar, esclava, librado en Caracas, en ratificación del que habia dado seis años antes," ibid.
29. "Juan de la Rosa y su mujer, Nicolasa Bolívar, con las instancias y demás diligencias relativas a su protocolización, hechas por Juan de la Rosa y María Jacinta Bolívar por su propio derecho"; cf. "El Libertador protocoliza en Caracas, a 26 de abril de 1817, la concesión de libertad a favor de sus propios esclavos, otorgada en 1821 después de la batalla de Carabobo" (Doc. 243), ibid., vol. 3, pp. 138–142.
30. "Decreto de Bolívar, fechado en Ceiba Grande el 23 de octubre de 1820, por el cual confisca la hacienda del mismo nombre y da libertad a sus esclavos," ibid., vol. 18, p. 584.
31. "Durante la campaña de 1814 ofrecio el Libor y dio la libertad a los esclavos que se presentaron a tomar las armas, y empezó por los suyos, de los cuales se presentaron como 15. Este decreto fue dado de Abril a Junio. En 1821 despues de Carabobo la dio generalmente y sin condicion a los esclavos de San Mateo cuyo no ignoro, po no bajaron de 100 y puede asegurarse q. eran mas. En esta vez lo hizo de palabra y cuando vino del Peru el año 1827 les otorgo escritura formal de libertad a los que vivian aun. Esto fue como particular a diferencia de lo del año de 14 que fue como majistrado qe disponia la cosa y daba el ejemplo de cumplir por su parte." This refers to the excerpt from a letter sent by Pedro Briceño Méndez, probably Bolívar's most trusted associate, in response to a question about the liberation of O'Leary's slaves: Robert Arthur Humphreys (ed.): *The "Detached Recollections" of General D. F. O'Leary* (London, 1969), p. 51.
32. "Poder especial conferido a su sobrino el capitán Anacleto Clemente," Caracas, 5 de julio de 1821 (Doc. 93), in *Escritos del Libertador*, vol. 2, pp. 247f.
33. Inés Quintero, "El inventario de los Bienes," in *La criolla principal* (Caracas, 2003), pp. 62–65.
34. The inventory itself has not come down to us. The most important data regarding the Bolívars' property and the inventory list are found in the correspondence between Simón and his sister María Antonia, in *Boletín de la Academia Nacional de la Historia*, no. 62 (1933): 265–298.
35. "Convenio celebrado entre el Libertador y su hermana María Antonia Bolívar," in *Papeles de Bolívar*, ed. Vicente Lecuna (Caracas, 1917), vol. 2, pp. 209–212, here p. 211. What Bolívar meant by that is explained by a letter he wrote from Guayaquil to Anacleto Clemente

on May 29, 1823: "Todos los esclavos que no eran del vínculo [de la Concepción], que tú posees ahora, los he dado por libres porque eran míos y he podido darles la libertad" (All slaves who were not on the Mayorazgo that you now own I have set free, because they were mine and I could give them their freedom); it is unclear whether or not Bolívar had the emancipation put in writing; see Document 118, in *Escritos del Libertador*, vol. 2, pp. 279ff. Turned around the other way, this means that for all the property from the family heritage that Clemente owned, slavery (now called "manumission")still held.

36. "Felicitaciones a la Señora Melchorana Toro, por el próximo matrimonia de su hija Rosa con Anacleto Clemente, sobrino del Libertador" (Doc. 95), in *Escritos del Libertador*, vol. 2, pp. 249f.
37. Letter from Bolívar to Anacleto Clemente, written October 9, 1821 from Rosario (Doc. 97), ibid., pp. 251f.
38. "Sargento Dioniso Bolívar, ex-esclavo de la familia cuyo apellido llevaba, según costumbre de la época, era en ese tiempo mayordomo del Libertador y se hallaba en Cúcuta." Cf. the footnote to Bolívar's letter to his "servant Dioniso," Guanare, May 24, 1821 (Doc. 92), ibid., pp. 246f.
39. "Testamento del Libertador," ibid., vol. 3, pp. 287–292, here p. 289.
40. Ibid.
41. José María Ots Capdequí, *España en América. El régimen de tierras en la época colonial* (México, 1959).
42. Michael Zeuske, "Eliten, Sklaverei und Land," in *Kleine Geschichte Venezuelas* (Munich, 2007), pp. 66–75.
43. "Convenio celebrado entre el Libertador y su hermana María Antonia Bolívar," in *Papeles de Bolívar*, ed. Vicente Lecuna (Caracas, 1917), vol. 2, pp. 209–212, here p. 210.
44. John V. Lombardi, "The Social Order of Venezuela: Property, Society, and Authority in Times of Bolívar, 1750–1850," in *Simón Bolívar: Persönlichkeit und Wirkung*, ed. Wilhelm Stegmann (Berlin, 1984), pp. 167–184.
45. Crisálida Dupuy, *Propiedades del general Juan Vicente Gómez, 1901–1935* (Caracas, 1983).
46. Michael Zeuske, "Simón Bolívar und die Unabhängigkeit (1800 bis 1859)," in *Kleine Geschichte Venezuelas* (Munich, 2007), pp. 42–101.
47. "Sentencia de Revista," in Vicente Lecuna (ed.): *Papeles de Bolívar*, ed. Vicente Lecuna (Caracas, 1917), vol. 2, pp. 208f., here p. 208.
48. "Convenio celebrado entre el Libertador y su hermana María Antonia Bolívar," ibid, pp. 209–212, here p. 211.
49. Inés Quintero, *La criolla principal* (Caracas, 2003), pp. 62–65.

50. Guárico is the old Spanish name for Santo Domingo/Haiti; Bolívar refers here to his fear of a slave revolt and free colored people.
51. "Por aqui se sabe poco del congreso y de Cúcuta; se dice que muchos en Cundinamarca quieren federación; pero me consuela con que ni Vd. ni Nariño, ni Zea, ni yo, ni Páez, ni otras muchas autoridades venerables que tiene el ejército libertador gustan de semejante delirio. Por fin, por fin han de hacer tanto los letrados, que se proscriban de la república de Colombia, como hizo Platón con los poetas en la suya. Esos señores piensan que la voluntad del pueblo es la opinión de ellos, sin saber que en Colombia el pueblo está en el ejército, porque realmente está, y porque ha conquistado este pueblo de mano de los tiranos; porque además es el pueblo que quiere, el pueblo que obra, y el pueblo que puede; todo demás es gente que vegeta con más o menos malignidad, o con más o menos patriotismo, pero todos sin ningún derecho a ser otra cosa que ciudadanos pasivos. Esta política, que ciertamente no es de la de Rosseau, al fin será necesario desenvolverla para que no nos vuelvan a perder esos señores. Ellos pretenden con nosotros representar el segundo acto de Buenos Aires, cuando la segunda parte que van a dar es la del Guárico. Piensan esos caballeros que Colombia está cubierta de lanudos, arropados en las chimeneas de Bogotá, Tunja y Pamplona. No han echado sus miradas sobre los caribes del orinoco, sobre los pastores del Apure, sobre los marineros de Maracaibo, sobre los bogas del Magdalena, sobre los bandidos de Patía, sobre los indómitos pastusos, sobre los guajibos de Casanare y sobre todas las hordas salvajes de Africa y de América que, como gamos, recorren las soledades de Colombia." Documents 5635–6154, May 14–August 31, in *Escritos del Libertador*, vol. 20, pp. 151ff., here p. 152; see also Marixa Lasso, "Introduction: The Wars of Independence," in idem, *Myths of Harmony: Race and Republicanism during the Age of Revolution, Colombia 1795–1831* (Pittsburgh, 2007), pp. 1–15.
52. Larry Herrera, "Bolívar, José," in *Diccionario de Historia de Venezuela*, ed. Manuel Rodríguez Campos, 4 vols. (Caracas, 1997), vol. 1, p. 477.
53. Francisco J. Ribas, *Elogio fúnebre que en obsequio del héroe granadino, el inmortal Girardot rinde reconocida Venezuela* (Caracas, 1813); Arístides Rojas, *El corazón de Girardot, 1813–1814: Un corazón que clama por sepultura, 1822–1891* (Caracas, 1891).
54. Narciso Coll y Prat, *Memoriales sobre la independencia de Venezuela* (Caracas, 1960).
55. *Título de Libertador y capitán general de los ejércitos de Venezuela por las autoridades y Municipalidad de Caracas en nombre de los*

pueblos al general Simón Bolívar (Caracas, 1813).
56. Ezequiel Urdaneta Braschi, hijo: "Medallas que se batieron y circularon en la vida del Libertador," in *Bolívar en la numismática conmemorativa y en las condencoraciones,* pref. J. L. Salcedo-Bastardo (Caracas, 1983), pp. 19–44; Enrique Uribe White, *Iconografía del Libertador* (Caracas, 1967).
57. Ministerio de Relaciones Exteriores (ed.), *Bolívar y Colombia: Bicentenario Natalicio del Libertador* (Bogotá, n.d.). The standard study on Bolívar iconography is Alfredo Boulton, *El Rostro de Bolívar* (Caracas, 1982); see the *Catálogo Iconográfico* on the Bolívar Web site of the Universidad de los Andes (Mérida), http://www.Bolívar.ula.ve (accessed December 12, 2010). See also Katherine E. Manthorne, *Tropical Renaissance: North American Artists Exploring Latin America, 1839–1879* (Washington, DC, 1989).
58. This is the starting point for the oral tradition. A few of the carvers of sacred images who, as we have said, often came from pardo families, might also have carved synecretistic figures of saints and thus begun the tradition of the "Pardo Bolívar" on the domestic altars of the colored urban population.
59. The painting attributed to Lovera was put on sale by Christie's in late 2010; see http://www.christies.com/LotFinder/lot_details.aspx?intobjectID=5316876 (accessed December 12, 2010).
60. Carlos V. Duarte, *Juan Lovera, el pintor de los procures* (Caracas, 1985).
61. Humboldt, writing from Teplitz to Bunsen, July 1,1830, in *Briefe von Alexander von Humboldt an Christian Carl Josias Bunsen,* ed. Ingo Schwarz (Berlin, 2006), pp. 21ff., here p. 22.
62. General Tomás Cipriano de Mosquera, along with Daniel Florencio O'Leary the "last Bolívarian," had already commissioned Tenerani to make the famous marble bust of Bolívar in the ancient Roman style now in the Casa Nariño in Bogotá; see Cipriano Rodríguez Santa María, "Der Bolívar Teneranis," in *Bolívar y "Colombia": bicentenario natalicio del Libertador,* ed. Ministerio de Relaciones Exteriores (Bogotá, 1983), pp. 25f.
63. Ana C. Ojeda Avellaneda, "Origen del hombre convertido en héroe," in *El mito Bolivariano en la literatura latinoamericana: Aproximaciones* (Bucaramanga, 2002), pp. 19–36, here pp. 25–33.
64. Pedro Calzadilla, "El olor de la pólvora: Fiestas patrias, memoria y Nación en la Venezuela guzmancista," *CHLB Caravelle,* no. 73 (1999), pp. 111–130.
65. Arturo Uslar Pietri, *Esquema de la historia monetaria venezolana* (Caracas, 1937); Alfonso Espinoza, *El bolívar, moneda nacional*

(Caracas, 1961); Marco Antonio Martínez, *Los nombres de las monedas en Venezuela* (Caracas, 1993). One peso fuerte (venezolano) = 5 francs (silver) or 1 bolívar = 1 franc (gold). See Friedrich Noback, *Münz-, Maass- und Gewichtsbuch: Das Geld-, Maass- und Gewichtswesen, die Wechsel- und Geldkurse, das Wechselrecht und die Usanzen* (Leipzig, 1877), p. 226.

66. Yolanda Salas de Lecuna, *Bolívar y la historia en la conciencia popular* (Caracas, 1987), p. 46.
67. "Bello, joven entonces de diez y ocho años, es presentado al viajero, quien puede calarle desde la primera conversación en francés que con aquel entabla. El prusiano, al ver cómo latía aquél corazón animado del sentimiento de lo bello y del amor a la naturaleza, estréchale la mano y le alienta con frases lisonjeras." Cf. Arístides Rojas, *Humboldtianas*, 2 vols. (Buenos Aires. 1942 (1st ed. 1924; collected journalism, 1879/80), vol. 2, p. 21. The articles may go back to a collection of memories that Rojas had published earlier; see idem, *Recuerdos de Humboldt* (Puerto Cabello, 1874); on Bello and the European canon, see Andrea Pagni, "Versiones y subversiones del canon europeo en el siglo XIX: Simón Rodríguez, Andrés Bello y Juan Antonio Pérez Bonalde," in *Nación y Literatura. Itinerarios de la palabra escrita en la cultura venezolana*, ed. Carlos Pacheco, Luis Barrera Linares, and Beatriz González Stephan (Caracas, 2006), pp. 153–175.
68. Kurt-R. Biermann, "War Alexander von Humboldt ein 'Freiherr' (oder 'Baron')?" in *NTM-Schriftenreihe Geschichte der Naturwissenschaft, Technik und Medizin* (Leipzig) 26, no. 2 (1989): 1ff.
69. On the background, see Gregory Zambrano, "Arístides Rojas y la memoria colectiva venezolana," in Arístides Rojas, *Orígenes Venezolanos: Historia, Tradiciones, Crónicas y Leyendas* (Caracas, 2008), pp. ix–lviii.
70. Ibid., p. xxi.
71. Gregory Zambrano, "Arístides Rojas y José Martí," in ibid., pp. xxv–xxviii.
72. Eduardo Blanco, *Venezuela heroica* (Caracas, 1981).
73. *Memorias del General O'Leary, publicadas por su hijo Simón B. O'Leary, por orden del gobierno de Venezuela y bajo los auspicios de su presidente General Guzmán Blanco, Ilustre Americano, Regenerador de la República*, 32 vols. (Caracas, 1882; repr. as *Memorias del General O'Leary, edición facsimilar del original de la primera edición, con motivo de la celebración del Sesquicentenario de la Muerte de Simón Bolívar, Padre de la Patria*, 34 vols. Caracas, 1981); Michael Zeuske, "Die 'Memorias del General o'Leary' und

der Bolívar-Kult: Politik und Geschichte am Beispiel der Bolívarquellen," *Asien, Afrika, Lateinamerika* (Berlin) 15, fasc. 6, (1987), pp. 1076–1081.
74. José Félix Blanco and Ramón Azpurúa (eds.), *Documentos para la historia de la vida pública del Libertador*, 16 vols. (Caracas, 1978).
75. Simón Bolívar, *Cartas del Libertador corregidas conforme a los originales*, ed. Vicente Lecuna, 11 vols. (Caracas, 1929–1939, 1954).
76. Vicente Lecuna (ed.), *Proclamas y discursos del Libertador, corregidos conforme a los originales* (Caracas, 1939); see also the shorter version: Simón Bolívar, *Obras Completas*, 3 vols. (Caracas, 1982).
77. Sociedad Bolivariana de Venezuela (ed.), *Escritos del Libertador*, 28 vols. (Caracas, 1964–1974).
78. Cristóbal Mendoza, *Escritos del Doctor Cristóbal Mendoza (1772 a 1829)* (Caracas, 1972).
79. Germán Carrera Damas, "El primer intento de modernización como busqueda de una salida a la crisis de la sociedad implantada," in *Una nación llamada Venezuela* (Caracas, 1997), pp. 91–117, here p. 104.
80. Josune Dorronsoro, "Historia capitulada de la fotografía en Venezuela," in *Visiones del oficio. Historiadores venezolanos en el siglo XXI*, ed. José Angel Rodríguez (Caracas, 2000), pp. 255–288.
81. Juan Calzadilla, *Martín Tovar y Tovar* (Caracas, 1977).
82. Ibid.
83. Leszek A. Zawisa, *Arquitectura y obras públicas en Venezuela, siglo XIX*, 3 vols. (Caracas, 1989).
84. Cornelis Goslinga, *Estudio biográfico y crítico de Arturo Michelena* (Maracaibo, 1967); María Capriles et al., *Arturo Michelena: Su obra y su tiempo* (Caracas, 1989); Rafael Pineda, *Iconografía de Francisco de Miranda: Retratos, estatuas y medallas; Algunos lugares, personas, hechos y cosas relacionados con su memoria* (Caracas, 2001). The Miranda submyth has recently also appeared in a film: Alejandro E. Gómez, "Las aventuras de Francisco de Munchausen," *Nuevo Mundo Mundos Nuevos: Imágenes en movimiento*, May 14, 2007, http://nuevomundo.revues.org/3920 (accessed March 26, 2011).
85. Ezequiel Urdaneta Braschi, hijo, *Bolívar en la numismática conmemorativa y en las condecoraciones* (Toledo, 1983), pp. 45ff. and passim.
86. Inés Quintero, "Bolívarismo y Gomecismo: La primera conmemoración de la muerte de Simón Bolívar en Europa," in *Bolívar y Europa en las crónicas, el pensamiento político y la historiografía*, ed. Alberto Filippi, 3 vols. (Caracas, 1986–1996), vol. 2, pp. 768–782.
87. Rafael Pineda, *La pintura de Tito Salas* (Caracas, 1974).

88. Vicente Dávila, *Archivo del general Miranda*, 24 vols. (vols. 1–15, Caracas, 1929–1938; vols. 16–24, Havana, 1950).
89. República de Venezuela, Ediciones de la Presidencia (ed.), *Itinerario Documental de Simón Bolívar: Escritos Selectos; Homenaje al Dr. Vicente Lecuna en el centenario de su nacimiento* (Caracas, 1970), flyleaf, p. i.
90. Ibid., p. ix.
91. Ibid.
92. Ibid.
93. Ibid.
94. Alberto Filippi (ed.), *Bolívar y Europa en las crónicas, el pensamiento político y la historiografía*, 3 vols. (Caracas, 1986–1996).
95. Vinicio Romero, *Diccionario del pensamiento Bolivariano: Ideas, frases y expresiones del Libertador* (Caracas, 1995); Octavio Arizmendi Posada and Carlos Gómez Botero, *Así pensaba Bolívar: Las mejores frases del Libertador presentadas por temas* (Bogotá, 2000).
96. Comité Regional Bicentenario del Natalicio del Libertador (Estado Miranda), *Decretos del Libertador*, 3 vols., Biblioteca de Autores y Temas Mirandinos (Los Teques 1983).
97. José León Tapia, *Maisanta: El último hombre a caballo* (Caracas, 1976; 7th ed. 2004).
98. Christine Hatzky, *Julio Antonio Mella (1903–1929): Eine Biografie*, Reihe Forum Iberoamericanum (Frankfurt am Main, 2004); idem, *Biografía de Julio A. Mella* (Havana, 2008).
99. Germán Carrera Damas, *Historiografía marxista y la emergencia de un líder: Rómulo Betancourt y el Plan de Barraquilla* (Caracas, 1994); Rafael Caldera et al., *Rómulo Betancourt: Historia y contemporaneidad* (Caracas, 1989); Manuel Caballero, "Del comunismo a la socialdemocracia a través del leninismo," in ibid., pp. 161–176.
100. Carlos Irazábal, *Hacia la Democracia* (México, 1939).
101. Tomás Straka, "Venezuela: Bolívarismo, socialismo y democracia; La historia como debate político (1939–1999)," *Tiempos de América. Revista de Historia, Cultura y Territorio*, no. 16 (1990): 63–83, here p. 72.
102. Inés Quintero, "Bolívar de izquierda, Bolívar de derecha: Nación y construcción discursiva," http://www.Simón-Bolívar.org/Principal/Bolívar/bolizbolder.html (accessed September 29, 2009); Inés Quintero and Vladimir Acosta, *El Bolívar de Marx* (Caracas, 2007).
103. Tomás Straka, "Venezuela: Bolívarismo, socialismo y democracia: La historia como debate político (1939–1999)," *Tiempos de América: Revista de Historia, Cultura y Territorio*, no. 16 (1990): 63–83, here p. 65.

104. A work primarily by Manfred Kossok and Max Zeuske, and to a lesser extent by Anatoli Shulgovskijs, see Max Zeuske, "Simón Bolívar und Karl Marx," in *Die Weltbühne* (Berlin, 1983), pp. 995–998; idem, "Simón Bolívar, su posición en la historia y en la actualidad," *Interpretaciones y ensayos marxistas acerca de Simón Bolívar*, ed. Max Zeuske (Berlin, 1985), pp. 1–20; Manfred Kossok, "Simón Bolívar, ¿el primer bonapartista de América Latina?" ibid., pp. 34–39; Manfred Kossok, "Simón Bolívar und das historische Schicksal Spanisch-Amerikas," in his *Ausgewählte Schriften*, ed. Matthias Middell, 3 vols. (Leipzig, 2000), vol. 2, pp. 251–272. My personal scholarly opinion is that Marx's article is largely worthless unless we read it in connection with Marx's debates with Bonapartism.
105. Federico Brito Figueroa, "Entrevista imaginaria con Laureano Vallenilla Lanz: 'Las revoluciones son fenómenos inevitables,' " in *30 ensayos de compresión histórica* (Caracas, 1991), pp. 1–19; idem, "Laureano Vallenilla Lanz y la compresión histórica de Venezuela colonial," ibid., pp. 21–54.
106. One of the great exceptions is the ethno-historian and anthropologist Acosta Saignes; Miguel Acosta Saignes, *Acción y utopía del hombre de las dificultades* (Havana, 1977); see also Tomás Straka, *La épica del desencanto* (Caracas, 2009).

Chapter III

1. "Que dites-vous de Miranda? Le jeune Bolívar en sera-t-il? Que de pendants! Vous verrez que cela finira mal." The reference is to a note written in tiny letters at the bottom of a letter from Humboldt to Bonpland dated June 27, 1806; see *Archives inédites de Aimé Bonpland*, pref. Henri Cordier, 2 vols. (Buenos Aires), vol. 1: *Lettres inédites de Alexandre de Humboldt* (Trabajos del Instituto de Botánica y Farmacologia/Facultad de Ciencias Médicas de Buenos Aires, no. 31), p. 36. See also Nicolas Hossard, *Alexander von Humboldt et Aimé Bonpland: Correspondance 1805–1858* (Paris, 2004).
2. Michael Zeuske, *Francisco de Miranda und die Entdeckung Europas:. Eine Biografie* (Hamburg, 1995); Michael Zeuske, "Francisco de Miranda (1750–1816): América, Europa und die Globalisierung der ersten Entkolonialisierung," in *Globale Lebensläufe: Menschen als Akteure im weltgeschichtlichen Geschehen*, ed. Bernd Hausberger (Vienna, 2006), pp. 117–142.
3. "De cette position naît une confusion d'idées et des sentiments inconcevables, une tendance révolutionnaire génerale. Mais ce désir

se borne à chasser les Européens et à se faire après la guerre entre eux." Cf. Margot Faak (ed.), *Humboldt, Lateinamerika am Vorabend der Unabhängigkeitsrevolution: Eine Anthologie von Impressionen und Urteilen aus den Reisetagebüchern* (Berlin, 1982), p. 64 (Dokument 1, written in Guayaquil between January 4 and February 17, 1803).

4. Charles Minguet, "Las relaciones entre Alexander von Humboldt y Simón Bolívar," in *Bolívar y Europa en las crónicas, el pensamiento político y la historiografía*, ed. Alberto Filippi, 3 vols. (Caracas, 1986–1996), vol. 1, siglo 19, pp. 743–754; see also Kurt R. Biermann, "Wer waren die wichtigsten Briefpartner Alexander von Humboldts?" in *Miscellanea Humboldtiana*, Beiträge zur Alexander-Von-Humboldt-Forschung, 15 (Berlin, 1990), pp. 230–236.

5. "Reciba Ud. los cordiales testimonio de quien ha tenido el honor de respetar su nombre antes de conocerlo, y de amarlo cuando lo vio en Paris y Roma." Letter from Bolívar to Humboldt, November 10, 1821, in Filippi (ed.), *Bolívar y Europa en las crónicas*, vol. 1, pp. 749f.

6. "La amistad con la cual se dignó honrarme después de mi regreso de México, en una época en que haciamos votos por la independencia y la libertad del Nuevo Continente." Letter from Humboldt to Bolívar, July 29, 1822, ibid., p. 749.

7. "Bolívar ... mereció en Paris [1804] su cariñosa amistad y aprovechó hasta cierto punto los consejos de su enorme sabiduría y consumada prudencia; quien era entonces tan aturdido, tan ligero, tan inconstante." Vicente Rocafuerte to Humboldt, London, December 17, 1824, in *Alexander von Humboldt, Cartas americanas*, ed. Charles Minguet (Caracas, 1980), pp. 270f., here p. 270.

8. This passage fundamentally contradicts Humboldt's entries in his diary.

9. This sentence could be modeled on the passage in Humboldt's letter cited above: "in der wir unsere Stimmen für die Unabhängigkeit und Freiheit des Neuen Kontinents erhoben."

10. Enigmatic: New Granada was called "Colombia" neither before 1810, the time about which Humboldt is supposed to be speaking here, nor in 1853; it was called "Nueva Granada." Only between 1819 and 1830/31 was part of the large country known by the name "Colombia"; the latter was reintroduced only in 1863, and it is still the name of the country today.

11. Günter Kahle, "Simón Bolívar und Alexander von Humboldt," in *Simón Bolívar und die Deutschen* (Berlin, 1980), pp. 39–49, here pp. 48f.

12. In O'Leary's account of his life there is no mention of a visit to Berlin in 1853. See Manuel Pérez Vila, *Vida de Daniel Florencio O'Leary* (Caracas, 1957); as well as Afonso Rumazo González, *O'Leary: Edecán del Libertador* (Caracas, 1978); Edgardo Mondolfi Gudat, *Daniel F. O'Leary*, Biblioteca Biográfica Venezolana, no. 28 (Caracas, 2006).
13. Manfred Kossok, "Alexander von Humboldt und der historische Ort der Unabhängigkeitsrevolution Lateinamerikas," *Alexander von Humboldt: Wirkendes Vorbild für Fortschritt und Befreiung der Menschheit; Festschrift aus Anlass seines 200. Geburtstages* (Berlin, 1969), pp. 1–26, here pp. 23f.
14. Hanns Heiman, "Humboldt und Bolívar. Begegnung zweier Welten in zwei Männern." in *Alexander von Humboldt: Studien zu seiner universalen Geisteshaltung*, ed. Joachim H. Schultze (Berlin, 1959), pp. 215–234, here pp. 233f.
15. Michael Zeuske, "Humboldt und Bolívar," in *Alexander von Humboldt: Netzwerke des Wissens* (catalog of the exhibit of the same name in Berlin, June 6–August 15, 1999 and Bonn September 15, 1999–January 9, 2000] Bonn/Munich/Berlin 1999, pp. 129f.; Michael Zeuske, "Vater der Unabhängigkeit? Humboldt und die Transformation zur Moderne im spanischen Amerika," in *Alexander von Humboldt: Aufbruch in die Moderne,* (Berlin, 2001), pp. 179–224.
16. Kurt-R. Biermann, "Aimé Bonpland im Urteil Alexander von Humboldts," *Miscellanea Humboldtiana* (1990), pp. 175–187, here p. 185; see also idem, "Alexander von Humboldt und Simón Bolívar.," in *Revista* (Dresden), no. 8 (1964): 26f.
17. Hanno Beck, "Hinweis auf Gespräche Alexander von Humboldts," in Heinrich Pfeiffer, *Alexander von Humboldt: Werk und Weltgeltung* (Munich, 1969), p. 265.
18. Cornelio Hispano, "Humboldt y Bolívar," in *El libro de oro de Bolívar* (Caracas, 2007), pp. 55–61, here pp. 59f., http://www.scrivol.com/doc/32483234/Cornelio-Hispano-El-Libro-de-oro-de-Bolívar (accessed November 26, 2010).
19. "Veintitrés años después de la muerte de Bolívar, en 1853, en una conferencia que por el orden del lord Clarendon tuvo con Humboldt, en Berlín, el general o'Leary, amigo y edecán que fue del Libertador, para tratar asuntos relacionados con la apertura de un canal interoceánico por el istmo del Darién, Humboldt, después de haber departido con su interlocutor sobre esta cuestión, habló en seguida de la América española y de Bolívar." Ibid., p. 59.
20. " 'Le traté mucho después de mi regreso de América, dijo, a fines de 1804.' " Ibid., pp. 59f.

21. Ibid., p. 267.
22. Charles Minguet, "Las relaciones entre Alexander von Humboldt y Simón Bolívar," in *Bolívar y Europa en las crónicas, el pensamiento politico y la historiografía*, ed. Alberto Filippi (Caracas, 1986), vol. 1, pp. 743–754, here pp. 751f. (Doc. 215). The precise reference is to Arístides Rojas, *Humboldtianas*, 2 vols. (Buenos Aires, 1942), vol. 2, pp. 179ff.
23. Ibid. The passage in Rojas corresponds to that quoted by Charles Minguet; Hispano varies the introduction somewhat. On the background, see Gregory Zambrano, "Arístides Rojas y la memoria colectiva venezolana," in Arístides Rojas, *Orígenes Venezolanos: Historia, Tradiciones, Crónicas y Leyendas* (Caracas, 2008), pp. ix–lviii.
24. Ibid.
25. Arístides Rojas, *Humboldtianas* (Caracas, 1900), pp. 179–181, here p. 181n.6.
26. Robert Arthur Humphreys (ed.), *The "Detached Recollections" of General D. F. O'Leary* (London, 1969), pp. 50f.
27. "Uno de sus encuentros en este viaje fue con el barón de Humboldt que nos había visitado pocos años antes, y preguntándole qué le parecía de su proyecto, le respondió aquel sabio: 'Yo creo que su país ya está maduro; mas no veo al hombre que pueda realizarlo.' ... Y lo tenía delante, pero él mismo no se conocía." Quoted from *Escritos del Libertador*, vol. 1, pp. 168f.; see also Charles Minguet, "Las relaciones entre Alexander von Humboldt y Simón Bolívar," p. 743; Cristóbal Mendoza and Javier Francisco Yanes (eds.), *Colección de documentos relativos a la vida pública del Libertador de Colombia y del Perú, Simón Bolívar para servir a la historia de Independencia de Sur América*, 21 vols. (Caracas, 1826–1829), vol. 1.
28. "Bolívar hablaba la lengua francesa con toda perfección y soltura, y en ella encontraba los términos más propios para expresar sus ideas sobre la indignidad de la vida colonial, sobre la libertad y la grandeza de los destinos futuros de América; y el baron le respondia: en efecto, Señor, creo que su país está ya en el caso de recibir la emancipación, pero ¿quién será el hombre que podrá acometer tan magna empresa? Teníalo delante y no lo adivinaba. Bolívar hubiera podido responderle: Ego sum qui loquor tecum...." Felipe Larrazábal, "La vida de Bolívar, Libertador de Colombia y del Perú, Padre y Fundador de Bolivia: Escrita cuidadosamente, con presencia de documentos auténticos y muchos indéditos, de grande interés," in *Correspondencia General del Libertador Simón Bolívar: Enriquecida con la inserción de los manifiestos, mensages, exposiciones, proclamas*, 2 vols. (New York, 1865), vol. 1, pp. 1–616; vol. 2, pp.

11–591; here vol. 1, p. 13.
29. Francisco Morales Padrón, *Rebelión contra la Compañía de Caracas* (Sevilla, 1955); Federico Brito Figueroa, *Las insurrecciones de los esclavos negros en la sociedad colonial venezolana* (Caracas, 1961); Carlos Felice Cardot, *Rebeliones, motines y movimientos de masas en el siglo XVIII venezolano (1730–1781)* (Caracas, 1977); Manuel Vicente Magallanes, *Luchas e insurrecciones en la Venezuela Colonial* (Caracas, 1983).
30. In Germany, this work is known chiefly as *Reise in die Aequinoctialgegenden des neuen Continents in den Jahren 1799, 1800, 1801, 1802, 1803 und 1804: Verfasst von Alexander von Humboldt und Aimé Bonpland*, 6 vols. (Stuttgart, 1815–1829).
31. "Para aquella época todos los hombres de la revolución de 1810 principiaban a despertar como espíritus progresistas." Arístides Rojas, "Recuerdos de Humboldt. Al doctor Adolfo Ernst," in *Humboldtianas, Recopiladas y publicadas por Röhl, Eduardo* (Caracas, 1924), pp. 1–29, here p. 14.
32. The original is written in French: "C'est avec une satisfaction bien vive que j'aurai l'honneur de recevoir Monsieur le Général O'Leary vendredi, le 22 à 1h, pour le remercier du bienveillant envoi d'une lettre du spirituel Mr Pentland et rafraîchir avec lui les souvenirs de mon illustre ami le Général Bolivar. Je [?], Monsieur, que le jour et l'heure puissent vous convenir, regrettant entièrement de ne pas pouvoir jouir plutôt [*sic*] de votre aimable et instructive conversation.... Agréez, je vous prie mon Général, l'hommage de ma haute considération avec laquelle j'ai l'honneur d'être / Votre t(rès) h(umble) et t(rès) o(béissant) serviteur / Alexandre de Humboldt." In MSS141, Libros raros y manuscritos de la Biblioteca Luis Ángel Arango, Bogotá; http://www.banrepcultural.org.
33. Diego Carbonell, *General O'Leary íntimo* (Caracas, 1937). The correspondence runs from March 7, 1828 to December 8, 1853.

Instead of a Conclusion

1. José Ángel Rodríguez, "El culto a Humboldt en Venezuela," http://www.uni-potsdam.de/u/romanistik/humboldt/hin/hin19/rodriguez.htm (accessed November 26, 2010).
2. Michael Zeuske, "Hugo Chávez Frías," in *Von Bolívar zu Chávez: Die Geschichte Venezuelas* (Zürich, 2008), pp. 420–436.
3. Frédérique Langue, "La Independencia de Venezuela, una historia mistificada y un paradigma histórico," in *Anuario de Estudios Amer-*

icanos 66, no. 2 (2009): 245–276; Michael Zeuske, "Una revolución con esclavos y con Bolívar: Un ensayo de interpretación," *Memorias: Revista Digital de Historia y Arqueología desde el Caribe* 8, no. 14 (June 2011), pp. 5–47. http://rcientificas.uninorte.edu.co/index.php/memorias/article/view/2006/1288.

4. Karin Gabbert, " 'Ein Held für alle Zwecke': Hugo Chávez und andere Wiedergänger von Simón Bolívar," *Jahrbuch Lateinamerika: Analysen und Berichte* 32 (2008): 156–165; Anne Huffschmid et al., *Erinnerung macht Gegenwart* (Münster, 2008).

5. Agustín Blanco Muñoz (ed.), *Habla el Comandante*, Serie "Testimonios Violentos" no. 12 (Caracas, 1998), pp. 58–80, here p. 58: [Chávez:] "Cuando fundamos el movimiento en el 82, siendo ya capitanes, era el EBR-200. Allí logramos darle un doble significado a las siglas: EBR, por Ezequiel Zamora, Bolívar y Rodríguez, en cuanto a la trilogía del árbol de las tres raíces." (When we founded the movement in 1982 [in reality, 1983—Z], being already captains, it was EBR-200. We were able to give the abbreviation a double meaning: EBR, for Ezequiel Zamora, Bolívar, and Rodriguez, in connection with the trilogy of the tree with three roots."). Hugo Chávez Frías, "Presencia del pensamiento de Zamora en el movimiento Bolívariano," *Últimas noticias* (Caracas), May 16, 1993, pp. 8f.

6. Elias Pino Iturrieta, *El divino Bolívar: Ensayo sobre una religión republicana*, Los libros de Catarata, 163 (Madrid 2003); also Harwich Vallenilla, "Introducción," in *Simón Bolívar, Estado ilustrado, nación inconclusa: La contradicción Bolívariana/Simón Bolívar, Estado ilustrado, nação inacabada: a contradição Bolívariana* (Madrid, 2004), pp. 1–61; see also the new analyses of the historical Bolívar and his familiar surroundings: Inés Quintero, *La criolla principal* (Caracas, 2003), passim; idem, *El último marqués: Francisco Rodríguez del Toro (1761–1851)* (Caracas, 2005).

7. An exception is the conservative Salcedo-Bastardo. José Luis Salcedo-Bastardo, *Simón Bolívar: Ein Kontinent und sein Schicksal* (Percha, 1978).

8. Günther Maihold, *Außenpolitik als Provokation: Rhetorik und Realität in der Außenpolitik unter Präsident Hugo Chávez* (Berlin, 2008) (= *SWP-Studie*, July 2008, p. 22).

9. Frédérique Langue, "La Independencia de Venezuela, una historia mistificada y un paradigma histórico," *Anuario de Estudios Americanos* 66, no. 2 (2009): 245–276; Domingo Irwin and Ingrid Micett, "De caudillos a pretorianos: Una Periodización de la realidad militar venezolana, siglos XIX y XX," *Nuevo Mundo Mundos Nuevos, Cuestiones del tiempo presente*, January 31, 2011, http://nuevo-

mundo.revues.org/60783 (accessed March 26, 2011).
10. Alejandro Gómez, "El papel de los intelectuales en la Venezuela de Hugo Chávez: Los historiadores a la palestra pública," *L'Ordinaire Latino-Américain* (Toulouse), no. 202 (October–December 2005): 83–94.
11. "El interés de la reescritura actual de la historia por el mismo presidente Chávez radica en el hecho de que Bolívar ya no es el aristócrata blanco (mantuano) o el defensor del orden que resultó ser hasta para ciertos autores europeos. Según varios defensores del régimen hasta se convirtió en un mestizo, más precisamente en un zambo." Frédérique Langue, "La Independencia de Venezuela, una historia mistificada y un paradigma histórico," *Anuario de Estudios Americanos* 66, no. 2 (2009): 245–276, here p. 255.
12. Michael Zeuske, *Kleine Geschichte Venezuelas* (Munich, 2007); idem, *Von Bolívar zu Chávez: Die Geschichte Venezuelas* (Zürich, 2008).
13. "La famosa escuela de samba Vila Isabel desfila con orgullo alrededor de una magnífica carroza de carnaval desde que se yergue hacia el cielo una figura impresionante, de doce metros de altura, vestida con una levita de color azul eléctrico engalanada con charretas y adornos dorados. El uniforme napoleónico, las patillas estilo imperio, las banderas tricolores amarillo-azul-rojo que lo acompañan no dejan lugar a dudas: es Simón Bolívar el personaje que encabeza la marcha, el hombre que liberó a un tercio del continente del yugo español y que soñó con verlo un día en una confederación libre y solidaria. A su alrededor, los sambistas avanzan a un ritmo frenético cantando en 'portuñol': Soy loco por tí América. La estatura del Libertador está acompañada por los retratos de San Martín, su homólogo argentino, del general brasileño Abreu Lima, que luchó en el ejército de Bolívar, de Tiradentes, precursor heroico de la independencia de Brasil, de Ernesto 'Che' Guevara, de Salvador Allende y de una media docena de glorias político-literarias como el cubano José Martí, el chileno Pablo Neruda y el poeta de la bossa nova Vinicius de Morães. Es el panteón heterogéneo de la izquierda continental." Marc Saint-Upéry, *El Sueño de Bolívar: El desafío de las izquierdas sudamericanas* (Barcelona, 2008), p. 11.

SELECT BIBLIOGRAPHY OF ENGLISH TEXTS ON SIMÓN BOLÍVAR

Bolívar, Simón. *El Libertador: Writings of Simón Bolívar*. Edited by David Bushnell. Translated by Fred Fornoff. New York: Oxford University Press, 2008.

Bushnell, David. *The Liberator, Simón Bolívar*. New York: Alfred A. Knopf, 2003. First published 1970.

Bushnell, David, and Lester D. Langley. *Simón Bolívar: Essays on the Life and Legacy of the Liberator*. Lanham, MD: Rowman & Littlefield, 2008.

Chasteen, John. "Simón Bolívar: Man and Myth." In *Heroes and Hero Cults in Latin America*, edited by Samuel Brunk and Ben Fallaw. Austin: University of Texas Press, 2006, pp. 21–39.

Collier, Simon. "Nationality, Nationalism and Supranationalism in the Writings of Simón Bolívar." *Hispanic American Historical Review* 63, no. 1 (1983): 37–64.

Ducoudray Holstein, H.L.V. *Memoirs of Simón Bolívar*. Boston: Goodrich, 1829. http://archive.org/details/memoirssimonbol00holsgoog (accessed May 2, 2012).

Earle, Rebecca. " 'Padres de la Patria' and the Ancestral Past: Commemorations of Independence in Nineteenth Century Spanish America." *Journal of Latin American Studies* 34, no. 4 (2002): 775–806.

———. " 'Sobre Heroes y Tumbas': National Symbols in Nineteenth Century Spanish America." *Hispanic American Historical Review* 85, no. 2 (2005): 375–416.

Harvey, Robert (2000). *Liberators: Latin America's Struggle for Independence, 1810–1830*. London: John Murray.

Lombardi, John V. "Epilogue: History and Our Heroes—The Bolívar Legend" and "Beginning to Read about Bolívar." In Bushnell and Langley, *Simón Bolívar: Essays*, pp. 159–191.

Lynch, John. *Simón Bolívar and the Age of Revolution*. London: University of London Institute of Latin American Studies, 1983.

———. *The Spanish American Revolutions, 1808–1826*. 2nd ed. New York: W. W. Norton, 1986.

———. *Simón Bolívar: A Life*. New Haven, CT: Yale University Press, 2007.

Madariaga, Salvador de. *Bolívar*. Westport: Greenwood Press, 1952.

Maher, John (ed.). *Francisco de Miranda: Exile and Enlightenment*. London: Institute for the Study of the Americas, 2006.

Marx, Karl. "Bolívar y Ponte" (1856). In *The New American Cyclopaedia: A Popular Dictionary of General Knowledge*, vol. 3. New York: D. Appleton, 1858 http://www.marxists.org/archive/marx/works/1858/01/bolivar.htm (accessed May 4, 2012).

Masur, Gerhard. *Simón Bolívar*. Rev. ed. Albuquerque: University of New Mexico Press, 1969.

Mijares, Augusto. *The Liberator*. Caracas: North American Association of Venezuela, 1983.

O'Leary, Daniel Florencio. 1888. *Bolívar and the War of Independence/ Memorias del General Daniel Florencio O'Leary: Narración*. Abridged ed. Austin: University of Texas, 1970.

Racine, Karen L. *Francisco de Miranda: A Transatlantic Life in the Age of Revolution*. Wilmington: SR Books (Latin American Silhouettes), 2003.

Slatta, Richard W., and de Grummond, Jane Lucas. *Simón Bolívar's Quest for Glory*. College Station, TX: Texas A&M University Press, 2003.

WORKS BY MICHAEL ZEUSKE ON BOLÍVAR, HUMBOLDT, MIRANDA, AND INDEPENDENCE

"Idea e intéres en la independencia." *Asien, Afrika, Lateinamerika* (*AALa*), special issue 14: "Interpretaciones marxistas de Simón Bolívar," ed. Max Zeuske. Berlin, 1985, pp. 40–49. Reprinted as "Acerca de la ilusión heroica en Simón Bolívar." In *Ensayos políticos acerca de Simón Bolívar*. Caracas, 2000, pp. 263–276.

"Miranda, Bolívar und San Martín und die kontinentale Komponente in der Independencia." *Leipziger Beiträge zur Revolutionsforschung* (*LBR*), edited by Manfred Kossok, vol. 14. Leipzig, 1985, pp. 27–46.

"El 'trienio liberal' en la obra de Simón Bolívar." In Albert Gil Novale (ed.). *La revolución burguesa en España*. Madrid, 1985, pp. 221–228.

"Simón Bolívar und das Verhältnis von Hegemonie und Triebkräften in der Independencia." *AALa* 14, no. 5 (1986): 880–894.

"Großkolumbien und die Befreiung Südamerikas: Kontinent und Region in der Revolutionskonzeption Simón Bolívars." *AALa* 15, no. 1 (1987): pp. 134–149.

"Die Memorias del General O'Leary und der Bolívar-Kult: Politik und Geschichte am Beispiel der Bolívar-quellen." *AALa* 15, no. 6 (1987): pp. 1076–1081.

"Bolívar y Europa." *Trienio: Ilustración y Liberalismo* (Madrid, edited by A. Gil Novales), no. 12 (Nov. 1988): 309–319.

"1789. School of Revolution: War and Politics in France and Spanish America; A Biographical Study of Francisco de Miranda." *AALa*, special issue 25 (1989): 27–38. Expanded and revised in German: "Francisco de Miranda: Eine biographische Studie." *Zeitschrift für Geschichtswissenschaft* 39, no. 5 (1991): 434–452.

"Francisco de Miranda ein venezolanischer General in der französischen Nordarmee (1792/93)." *Zeitschrift für Militärgeschichte* (Berlin), no. 1 (1989): 12–20.

"'Gott regiert im Himmel, auf Erden wir': Bemerkungen zum Verhältnis von Revolution und Religion im Werk von Simón Bolívar." *AALa* 17, no. 1 (1989): 112–121. Spanish version: "Revolución y religión: problemas de la religión en la concepción de la revolución en Simón Bolívar." In *Iglesia, religión y sociedad en la historia latinoamericana, 1492–1945: Protocolo del VIII Congreso de la Asociación de Historiadores Latinoamericanistas de Europa (AHILA)*, 4 vols. Szeged, 1989, vol. 3, pp. 203–216.

"'Heroische Illusion' und Antiillusion bei Simón Bolívar: Überlegungen zum Ideologiekomplex in der Independencia 1810–1830." In *1789 Weltwirkung einer großen Revolution*, edited by Manfred Kossok and Editha Kross. 2 vols. Berlin, 1989, vol. 2, pp. 577–596.

"Kolonialpolitik und Revolution: Kuba und die Unabhängigkeit der Costa Firme, 1808–1821; Reflexionen zu einem Thema der vergleichenden Revolutionsgeschichte." *Jahrbuch für Geschichte von Staat, Wirtschaft und Gesellschaft Lateinamerikas (JbLA)* (Cologne/Vienna) 27 (1990): pp. 149–198.

"Venezuela y Colombia: Revolución y guerras de independencia, 1810–1830." *Historia del ciclo de las revoluciones de Espana y América Latina (1790–1917)*, edited by Manfred Kossok and Sergio Guerra Vilaboy. Havana, 1990, pp. 26–31.

With Bernd Schröter: "Napoleon und Spanisch-Amerika: Transatlantische Wirkungen." In Napoleon und die nationale Unabhängigkeit: Der Widerspruch des Fortschritts, edited by Helmut Bock and Richard Plöse. Studien zur Geschichte, vol. 6. Berlin 1990, pp. 156–171.

"Don Francisco de Miranda: Biografía y cultura política (1772–1816)." *Apuntes: Revista Universitaria para Problemas de la Historia y la Cultura Iberoamericana* (Leipzig), n.s., no. 1 (1991), pp. 3–34.

"'Kommentare im Falsett': Medien, Nachrichten und Revolution am Beispiel der Independencia Venezuelas." *Comparativ*, fasc. 3 (1991): 54–68.

"Las Memorias del General O'Leary y el culto a Bolívar: Anotaciones sobre la relación entre política e historia en las fuentes Bolívarianas." *Hispanorama* (Nuremberg) 58 (June 1991): pp. 26–29.

"Variationen eines Themas: Die Transformation in Spanisch-Amerika, Vorwort des Herausgebers." *Comparativ: Leipziger Beiträge zur Universalgeschichte und zur vergleichenden Gesellschaftsforschung*, fasc. 2 (1991): 1–4.

With Manfred Kossok: "El factor militar en la Independencia: La dialectica entre guerra y revolución en el período 1810–1830." In *Les Révolutions Ibériques et Ibéro-Americaines à l'aube du XIXe siècle: Actes du colloque de Bordeaux 2–4 Juillet 1989*. Collection de la Maison des Pays Ibériques, 49. Paris, 1991), pp. 395–414.

With Bernd Schröter: "Das 'Gesetz der Franzosen' gegen 'frei und nicht französisch': Wirtschaftsregionen, Volksbewegungen und Radikalismus in Spanisch-Amerika: Überlegungen zum außereuropäischen Jakobinismus." In *Jakobinismus und Volksbewegung zur Zeit der Französischen Revolution*. Dem Wirken Walter Markovs gewidmet, Berlin 1991 (Sitzungsberichte der Akademie der Wissenschaften in Berlin, 1990), pp. 157–180.

With Bernd Schröter: "Transformation, Widerstand und Volksbewegungen in Spanisch-Amerika: Vom 'bourbonischen Jahrhundert' zur Unabhängigkeit." *Comparativ*, fasc. 2 (1991): 26–49.

"Alexander von Humboldt und das Problem der Transformation in Spanisch-Amerika: Texte Humboldts über die politische Mentalität amerikanischer oligarchien (speziell Kuba und Venezuela)." In *Alexander von Humboldt und das neue Geschichtsbild von Lateinamerika*, edited by Michael Zeuske and Bernd Schröter. Leipzig, 1992), pp. 145–215.

"América y Humboldt: El modelo de reformas alemanas y las realidades americanas; Una aproximación." In IX Congreso de Historia de América, *Europa e Iberoamérica: Cinco siglos de intercambios*, edited by María J. Sarabia Viejo, 3 vols. Seville, 1992, vol. 3, pp. 351–364.

With Bernd Schröter: "Vom 'bourbonischen Jahrhundert' zur Unabhängigkeit: Alexander von Humboldt und das neue Geschichtsbild von Lateinamerika." In *Alexander von Humboldt und das neue Geschichtsbild von Lateinamerika*, edited by Michael Zeuske and Bernd Schröter. Leipzig, 1992, pp. 10–15.

"¿Del 'buen gobierno' al 'mejor gobierno'? Alejandro de Humboldt y el problema de la transformación en América española." *Apuntes*, n.s., no. 1 (1993): pp. 1–86.

"Rasgos principales de la imagen de Bolívar en la RDA." In Alberto Filippi (ed.), *Bolívar y Europa en las crónicas, el pensamiento político y la historiografía*, 3 vols. Caracas, 1986–1996, vol. 3, pp. 167–183.

Francisco de Miranda und die Entdeckung Europas: Eine Biografie. Hamburg/Münster, 1995.

"Humboldt y el problema de la transformación en Venezuela y Cuba: Ocho tesis y un apéndice teórico (1760–1830)." In Alberto Gil Novales, *Ciencia e independencia política*. Madrid, 1996, pp. 83–129.

"Humboldt und Bolívar." In Alexander von Humboldt: Netzwerke des

Wissens (Katalog zur gleichnamigen Ausstellung in Berlin 6. Juni bis 15. August 1999 und Bonn 15. September 1999 bis 9. Januar 2000). Bonn/ München/Berlin, 1999, pp. 129f.

"¿Padre de la Independencia? Humboldt y la transformación a la modernidad en la América española." *Cuadernos Americanos* (México), no. 78 (1999): 20–51.

"¿Padre de la Independencia? Humboldt y la transformación a la modernidad en la América española." *Debate y perspectivas: Cuadernos de Historia y Ciencias Sociales*, special issue, "Alejandro de Humboldt y el mundo hispánico: La Modernidad y la Independencia americana," edited by Miguel Ángel Puig-Samper, no. 1 (December 2000): pp. 67–100.

"Alexander von Humboldt: Vergleiche und Transfers, Pantheons und nationale Mythen sowie Revolutionen und Globalisierungen (Einleitung)." In *Humboldt in Amerika*, edited by Michael Zeuske. Leipzig, 2001. Reprinted in *Comparativ*, fasc. 2 (2001): 7–15.

"'Geschichtsschreiber von Amerika': Alexander von Humboldt, Deutschland, Kuba und die Humboldteanisierung Lateinamerikas." In Humboldt in Amerika, edited by Michael Zeuske. Leipzig, 2001. Reprinted in *Comparativ*, fasc. 2 (2001): 30–83.

"Humboldt, Historismus, Humboldteanisierung." *Humboldt im Netz* 2, no. 3 (pt. 1.), (2001), http://www.unipotsdam.de/u/romanistik/humboldt/hin/hin3.htm.

"Vater der Unabhängigkeit? Humboldt und die Transformation zur Moderne im spanischen Amerika." In *Alexander von Humboldt. Aufbruch in die Moderne*, edited by Ottmar Ette, Ute Hermanns, Bernd Scherer, and Christian Suckow. Beiträge zur Alexander-von-Humboldt-Forschung, vol. 21. Berlin, 2001, pp. 179–224.

"Humboldt, Historismus, Humboldteanisierung." *Humboldt im Netz* 3, no. 4 (pt. 2), (2002), http://www.unipotsdam.de/u/romanistik/humboldt/hin/hin_4.htm.

"¿Humboldteanización del mundo occidental? La importancia del viaje de Humboldt para Europa y América Latina." *Humboldt im Netz* 4, no. 6 (2003), http://www.unipotsdam.de/u/romanistik/humboldt/hin/hin6/zeuske.htm.

"Regiones, espacios e hinterland en la independencia de Venezuela: Lo espacial en la política de Simón Bolívar." *Revista de las Américas: Historia y presente (RAs)*, no. 1 (spring 2003): pp. 39–58.

"Comparando el Caribe: Alexander von Humboldt, Saint-Domingue y los comienzos de la comparación de la esclavitud en las Américas."

Estudos Afro-Asiáticos (Rio de Janeiro), vol. 26, no. 2, (2004): pp. 381–416.

"Introducción." in Francisco de Miranda y la modernidad en América, introducción, selección, transcripción y notas de Michael Zeuske. Madrid, 2004 (Prisma Histórico: Viejos documentos, Nuevas lecturas; Velhos Documentos, Novas Leituras), pp. 13–106.

"'Real time': Humboldt und Kuba 1801 und 1804." In Michael Zeuske, *Schwarze Karibik, Sklaven, Sklavereikultur und Emanzipation*. Zürich, 2004, pp. 340–347.

"Alexander von Humboldt y la comparación de las esclavitudes en las Américas." *Humboldt im Netz* 6, no. 11 (2005): 65–89, http://www.unipotsdam.de/u/romanistik/humboldt/hin/hin11/inh_zeuske.htm.

"Regiones, espacios y hinterland en la Independencia: Lo regional en la política de Simón Bolívar." *Colectivos sociales y participación popular en la Independencia Hispanoamericana*, edited by Germán Cardozo Galué and Arlene Urdaneta Quintero. Maracaibo, 2005, pp. 147–162.

"Cuba, la esclavitud atlántica y Alexander von Humboldt: ¿de mal ejemplo a modelo de globalización eficaz?" In *La excepción americana: Cuba en el ocaso del imperio continental*, edited by Imilcy Balboa and José A. Piqueras. Valencia, 2006, pp. 21–35.

"Deutsche als Eliten in Lateinamerika (19. Jahrhundert): Regionen, Typen, Netzwerke und paradigmatische Lebensgeschichten." In *Deutsche Eliten in Übersee (16. bis frühes 20. Jahrhundert): Büdinger Forschungen zur Sozialgeschichte 2004 und 2005*, edited by Markus A. Denzel. Deutsche Führungsschichten in der Neuzeit, vol. 27. St. Katharinen, 2006, pp. 173–206.

"Francisco de Miranda (1750–1816): América, Europa und die Globalisierung der ersten Entkolonialisierung." In Globale Lebensläufe: Menschen als Akteure im weltgeschichtlichen Geschehen, edited by Bernd Hausberger. Vienna, 2006, pp. 117–142.

"Der andere Entdecker: Alexander von Humboldt; 'Wie unwirthbar macht Europäische Grausamkeit die Welt.'" *In Kolonialismus hierzulande: Eine Spurensuche in Deutschland*, edited by Ulrich van der Heyden and Joachim Zeller. Erfurt, 2008, pp. 90–94.

"Humboldt, esclavitud, autonomismo y emancipación en las Américas, 1791–1825." In *Alexander von Humboldt: Estancia en España y viaje americano*, edited by María no Cuesta Domingo and Sandra Rebok. Madrid, 2008, pp. 257–277.

"Arango y Humboldt/Humboldt y Arango: Ensayos científicos sobre la esclavitud." In María Dolores González-Ripoll and Izaskun Álvarez Cuartero. *Francisco de Arango y la invención de la Cuba azucarera*, edited by Aquilafuente, 158. Salamanca, 2009, pp. 245–260.

"Historia social precedente, historicismo marxista y el carácter de ciclo de las revoluciones: La obra de Manfred Kossok." In *La Ilusión heroic: Colonialismo, revolución, independencias en la obra de Manfred Kossok*, edited by Lluis Roura and Manuel Chust. Colleció Amèrica, 20. Castelló de la Plana, 2010, pp. 63–97.

"Michael Zeuske." In *Las independencias iberoamericanas en su laberinto: Controversias, cuestiones, interpretaciones*, edited by Manuel Chust. Valencia, 2010, pp. 375–390.

"Alexander von Humboldt in Cuba, 1800/01 and 1804: Traces of an enigma." *Studies in Travel Writing* 15, no. 4 (December 2011): 347–358.

"La Independencia 1810–1824: Unvollendete Revolution mit Sklaverei." In *"Lust am Krimi": Beiträge zu Werk und Wirkung Walter Markovs*, edited by Mathias Middell. Leipzig, 2011, pp. 187–241.

"Miranda, Bolívar y las construcciones de la 'independencia': Un ensayo de interpretación." In *Las independencias de Iberoamérica,* edited by Tomás Straka, Andrés Agustín Sánchez, and Michael Zeuske. Caracas, 2011, pp. 279–326.

"Nation und Revolution: Der Fall Venezuela." In *Nation und Revolution: Ernst Engelberg und Walter Markov zum 100. Geburtstag*, edited by Wolfgang Küttler and Matthias Middell. Geschichtswissenschaft und Geschichtskultur im 20. Jahrhundert, vol. 11. Leipzig, 2011, pp. 65–110.

"Una revolución con esclavos y con Bolívar: Un ensayo de interpretación." *Memorias: Revista Digital de Historia y Arqueología desde el Caribe* 8, no. 14 (June 2011): 5–47, http://rcientificas.uninorte.edu.co/index.php/memorias/article/view/2006/1288.

ABOUT THE AUTHOR AND TRANSLATOR

Michael Zeuske is Professor of Iberian and Latin American History at the University of Cologne in Germany. After taking a doctorate at the University of Leipzig, he was appointed Professor of Comparative History and Iberian-American History at the same university. In 1993, he was appointed to a chair at Cologne. Zeuske is one of the best-known scholars writing on Latin American history, especially the history of Cuba, Venezuela, and the Caribbean.

Steven Rendall is the freelance translator of more than sixty books from French and German. He has won the National Jewish Book Council's Sandra Brand and Arik Weintraub Award and the Modern Language Association's Scaglione Prize for his translations, and he was a finalist for the 2012 French-American Foundation translation award. He is also Professor Emeritus of the University of Oregon and Editor Emeritus of the journal *Comparative Literature*. He lives on a farm in southwest France with his wife, two dogs, three cats, and five chickens.

CPSIA information can be obtained at www.ICGtesting.com
Printed in the USA
BVOW080747251012

303912BV00002B/4/P